The Philosophy of Design

One idea is that design is not merely action of any old sort, but a specific kind of action: action that changes the world. The design theorist Christopher Jones, for example, suggested a definition of design as the intentional initiation of change (Jones 1970, 6).[8] For this definition to be an improvement on our first candidate, however, we'll need to understand the phrase "changes the world" in a substantive way: after all, any action at all changes the world in *some* way. If you bake a pie, for instance, then the world has one more pie in it than it did before. One way to construe "changing the world" in a more substantive way is to take it to mean bringing a new *sort of thing* into being. On this view, baking a pie does not really change the world, because it doesn't bring a new sort of thing into being – it simply adds one more of an existing type. On the other hand, when a new device, such as the iPod, or the Eames chair, is created, the world is altered in a substantial way – it is different than it was before.

Adopting Jones's suggestion, then, let us define "design" as the intentional creation of a new kind of thing. This definition brings us closer to the meaning of the contemporary concept of design, but it too is inadequate in two respects. First, the definition is too broad. Consider the members of a construction crew that builds an office tower: they create the structure, in a sense, but they do not design it. Designing a structure like an office tower is typically the job of someone else – the architect: workers assemble the required parts in the way the architect directs. That certainly involves skill, and may call for "on-the-spot" decisions about certain features not explicitly specified in the architect's plans. Nonetheless, it isn't the same as designing the structure. The problem here is that our definition allows for change that is achieved without any creativity or invention. We can fix this by amending our definition to "the intentional creation of *plans* for a new kind of thing" (cf. Love 2002).[9] Adding this necessary condition highlights the fact that design is essentially a conceptual or mental activity, distinct from the physical activity of making or building. Even if the structure that he has planned is never actually built, the architect has nevertheless designed something.[10]

Our definition still needs a second refinement, however. Say that Bill is creating plans for a new type of car, with the aim of reducing the size of the engine. In arranging the engine parts in a new way, he finds that, much to his surprise, the new engine runs at twice the normal efficiency. Bill acted intentionally in creating the new engine. However, Bill never intended to produce an engine with increased efficiency – in fact, improving efficiency never entered into his thinking at all, and this was a completely accidental discovery. Reflecting on this case, we might say that Bill *invented* or *discovered* the high-efficiency engine, but not that he *designed* it. The concept of design, it seems, entails a certain kind of rational connection between the final product and the creative process: if a person designs an X, then the creation of the plan for X is guided by the goal of producing something that can do what X does. To capture the concept of design, then, we will need to build this necessary condition into our definition somehow.

One way to do this is to construe design as, necessarily, a problem-solving activity.[11] The design process is not merely the production of plans for something new; rather, it is the production of such plans via the working-out of a potential solution to some problem. Based on such considerations, the philosopher Greg Bamford (1990, 234) offers a definition of the activity of "design" along the following lines:

Someone designs thing X at time t if and only if:

1. She imagines or describes X at t
2. While supposing that X at least partially satisfies some set of requirements R under conditions C and
3. Satisfying R is a problem for which
4. X is a novel or original solution

According to Bamford, these four conditions are individually necessary and jointly sufficient for the activity of design. We can gloss his definition in simpler language as follows: design is the intentional solution of a problem by the creation of plans for a new sort of thing.[12] Given this definition of the verb, we can now define the noun "design" simply as the problem-solving plan generated by this activity.[13]

A final point needs clarification, however. Above, we said that design is the mental activity of creating plans to solve a problem, and that this mental activity is distinct from the physical act of making. However, perhaps things are not quite so simple. Consider a person who draws up plans for a time machine. The plans specify various components, with various functions, such as "space–time continuum disruptor," "materialization point locator" and so on, although they do not describe how these components are to be built. This seems to fit our definition of "design" exactly: the inventor supposes that his planned device "would be such as to satisfy the requirements" of a time machine. But, intuitively, this hardly seems like a bona fide case of design.[14]

At a first glance, the problem seems to be that the design is not a genuine design for a time machine simply because it isn't a solution to the relevant problem at all – it doesn't work. However, this is not really the issue, since there are many bona fide cases of design for things that, when constructed, do not work. We do not want to say that someone who draws up plans for a lemon juicer that can't juice a lemon properly is not designing: what we should say is that he designs, but poorly.[15] The problem with the time machine case is not that the plan does not work, but that it is so implausible that any reasonable person can see immediately that it will not work. In short, this seems more like a case of *imagining* a time machine than *designing* one. Let us revise our definition a final time, then, as follows:

> Design is the intentional solution of a problem, by the creation of plans for a new sort of thing, where the plans would not be immediately seen, by a reasonable person, as an inadequate solution.

Note that, when applied to the juicer case mentioned above, this yields the correct result: the juicer, it turns out, fails as a solution, but its failure would not be immediately obvious in the way that the failure of the time machine is. Hence it counts as design.

The addition of this final constraint requires a few comments. First, we need to distinguish plans that are obviously inadequate *in principle* from plans that are hopeless for practical reasons, such as time constraints, the expense involved or the rarity of necessary materials. Only the former cases would fail to satisfy our constraint: a design for a device that was simply too expensive to construct would still be design. Second, the constraint that we have imposed on design is quite minimal: it does not require that the designer have any particular level of justification for thinking that his design will work. It only requires that the design not be a "non-starter," as it were.

This last feature means that we can now evaluate designs based on the level of justification available for belief in the likely success of the design: designs that may reasonably be thought likely to succeed can be called more rational than those for which the expected probability of success, given the available evidence, is smaller (Houkes and Vermaas 2010, 41; see also Hilpinen 2011). When the expected chance of success falls below a certain level, designing may become tantamount to the proverbial shot in the dark. As we will see in chapter 2, the extent to which designing can be considered a rational activity is one of the central issues for the philosophy of design.

1.2   Ontological Issues

Our definition raises some intriguing questions about the nature of design. One has to do with the product of the design process: just what sort of thing is it that designers produce? This is what philosophers call an *ontological* question, a question involving distinctions between different types of being.[16] What do we mean here by "types of being?" In one sense, there are a zillion different types of beings: cats, protons, cities, milkshakes and so on. But when philosophers talk about "types of beings" they have in mind certain very general categories into which such particular things fall. For instance, the things just mentioned are all what philosophers call *substances*: particular things that can be conceived to exist independently of anything else. For example, it is possible to conceive that the only thing that exists is a single cat.[17] In this regard, substances can be contrasted with entities falling into the ontological category of *property*, such as redness or squareness. We cannot conceive these existing independently of anything else: if redness or squareness exists, then there must be something else, something that has the property (that is, something that is red or square). Thus, philosophers place properties in a separate ontological category.

Ontology crops up, with respect to our definition of "design," in the following question: what exactly counts as "a new thing?" Sometimes, a designer might solve a problem by creating a plan, not so much for a new object, as for new *uses* for existing ones. Bamford offers the following example. "Consider . . . the rehoused Italian peasant, mystified by the w.c. in his modern flat, who surmises that the cistern can be used to cure olives. Should this peasant be counted as having designed an olive curer?" (1990, n32). Bamford answers "yes," despite the fact that the cistern is not modified in any way by the peasant. There is something odd, however, about saying that the peasant has designed an olive curer. The reason is that, in a sense, he hasn't created a new *thing*: he is just using an already existing thing. A better way to handle this example is to distinguish between two ontological categories: things and processes. Whereas things are particular substances, processes are causally related series of events. It is more accurate to say that the peasant hasn't designed an olive curer (a thing), but rather a new method for curing olives (a process).[18]

Another ontological distinction relevant to our definition is that between *types* and *tokens*. A type is a general kind, and a token of that type is a particular thing that is an instance of the type. Distinguishing types from tokens is often helpful in avoiding ambiguity and confusion. Consider, for instance, the number of words in this sentence: "The man held the cat." If we count by tokens, there are five, but if we count by types, only four, since there are two tokens of the word "the" in the sentence. In philosophy, the distinction between token and type becomes important in attempts to understand certain kinds of creative activity, such as art (Davies 2003).

In some of the arts, it seems that artworks are types, of which there can be multiple token instances. In musical composition, for example, it is natural to think of what the composer produces as a general type of sound structure (specified in a score), which we then find manifested in many particular performances, each of which is an equally legitimate token of the work (Sharpe 2004, 54–63). In other arts, however, such as sculpture and painting, this seems not to be the case. Here the work created is often a particular thing – a particular painted canvas or piece of shaped marble – rather than a general type. This is evident in the fact that we do not view an exact reproduction of such works as having the same value as the original. A copy of Picasso's painting *Guernica* is not a work of art made by Picasso; it is only a copy of one (and we treat it very differently as a result). This is not true of musical works – when you hear a contemporary performance of Beethoven's 7th symphony, you are not merely hearing a copy of an artwork by Beethoven: you are hearing an artwork by Beethoven.

In distinguishing these two kinds of artworks, it is somewhat awkward to refer to paintings and sculptures of the sort just described as tokens, rather than types. This is because merely calling them "tokens" suggests a general type of which they are instances, whereas for these works there really is no such type. Thus philosophers prefer to distinguish between *singular* and *multiple* works of art: multiple works can be realized, or instantiated, in multiple particular things at one time, whereas singular works can exist only as one particular object.

With respect to design, an analogous ontological question arises: are designs singular, like most sculptures, or multiply realizable, like musical scores? Since design is the production of a plan for something, and such plans can, in general, typically be implemented multiple times, an intuitive view is that designs are always multiply realizable (Dilworth 2001). In discussing his definition of "design," however, Bamford offers a different view. He writes:

> Some designs are designs for a particular thing, for example, an arrangement of freshly picked flowers. Further, only one arrangement of these flowers is possible at any one time. Other designs are type designs, for example, the design of [the Australian automobile] the Holden Commodore. From this type, many tokens can be made – all of which may exist at one time and satisfy [the requirements]. (1990, 234)

Although he employs different terminology, Bamford's comments suggest the view that some designs are singular, whereas others are multiple. Is he right?

It is certainly true that some designs are made with the intention that they be realized in particular materials, as in the flower example Bamford describes. In other cases, the designer may have no particular material in mind; any bit of steel will do to make a Holden Commodore, as long as it meets the appropriate functional requirements.

However, intentions are not decisive here. Commenting on the case of art, Stephen Davies observes that "no dramatist, simply by willing it, could make his play a singular work if it were scripted in the orthodox way" (2003, 159). That is, a playwright could insist all he liked that only one performance of his play counts as the work, and all others are mere copies; this would not change the fact that his play is a multiple work. Rather, a work can be singular only if there is a recognized social convention to this effect, as there is for works of sculpture and painting. In the case of flower designs, there do not seem to be such conventions: even if I design a certain flower arrangement for *these* particular flowers in front of me (perhaps because the design shows these particular flowers at their best), what I create is still a type (imagine someone seeing my arrangement and then using it to produce a whole series of table arrangements for a wedding). This arrangement can, just like an automobile design, be used to produce many tokens, all of which can exist at once and all of which are equally legitimate instances of the design. This example, then, does not refute the conception of the designer as a producer of plans that are, like novels and musical scores, essentially *multiply realizable*.[19]

Other examples that threaten this conclusion, however, can readily be found if we turn to architecture and designs for buildings. Many, perhaps most, building designs are multiply realizable: designs for family dwellings and commercial buildings are typically mass-produced, for example. However, things may be different if we consider plans worthy of description as "architectural works," rather than "mere buildings."[20] Some have argued that, in general, architectural works are singular: there can be only one instance of the work, and any other instantiation of the plan is a copy, not an instance of the work (see Davies 2003, 158; De Clercq 2012). This may not be true of all architectural works: consider kitHAUS, a mass-produced modular housing unit (Lopes 2007, 79). These cases notwithstanding, architecture does seem to offer plenty of examples of designs that are singular, rather than multiple in nature. In support of this view, Rafael De Clercq observes that "the names we associate with architectural works (e.g., 'the Seagram building' or 'the Pantheon') refer to concrete buildings, not to abstract designs. In this respect, architecture is unlike music, where the well-known names (e.g., 'Beethoven's *Fifth*') refer to abstract works rather than to particular performances of these works" (De Clercq 2012, 211). Extending De Clercq's point, we can note that a similar distinction exists between names for architectural works and names for every-day design items, such as the iPod or the Eames chair. When we talk about "*the* iPod," or "*the* Eames chair," we mean the type, not some particular individual object. But when we talk about architecture, it appears, the reverse is true, suggesting that only some designs are multiple.

However, De Clercq's point is not decisive, since the fact that everyday names for architectural works pick out particular, concrete objects can be explained without appealing to the singular nature of their designs. An obvious reason why we talk about a specific object in connection with the Seagram building or the Pantheon is that there happens to exist only one token of each of these design types. Indeed, this is the usual situation in architecture (Wicks 1994), in contrast to other areas of design: if only one Eames chair had been produced, then "the Eames chair" might also refer to a single particular object. But the fact that architectural designs are only realized once does not entail that they are singular: a musical work that happens to be performed only one time, and then never again, is not a singular work, since it remains capable of being multiply realized. The real issue, therefore, is what we would say *if* someone implemented the plans for, say, the Seagram building in another location. Robert Wicks refers to such reimplementation of original plans as a "refabrication" (1994). Our question, then, is: would a refabrication be another Seagram building, or a mere copy of the Seagram building?

This is a difficult question to answer, but it is clear that much would depend on the details of this imagined construction (or reconstruction). If features of the original that were not specified in the original plans (post-construction modifications to the first building, for example) were replicated, or if the motive behind the refabrication was to siphon tourist interest in the "original" Seagram building, then we might declare the second building a copy.[21] On the other hand, in the absence of such intentions, it is far from clear that the refabrication would be a mere copy. Imagine, for example, that the two buildings are created by the same construction team, using the same plans and materials, but only a short time apart. In this case we would hardly consider the second building a copy of the first. Now imagine that the builders are different, but equally skilled, and that one team builds ten years after the first: do we have any additional reason to view the second building as merely a copy of the first (Wicks 1994, 164)? In other words, it is far from clear that there is a convention concerning architectural design plans that renders them singular. Perhaps then, the view that architectural designs are multiply realizable, akin to musical scores, is feasible after all (Wicks 1994).

Stephen Davies, however, offers an argument for the view that at least some architectural designs are singular. This is because, he says, such buildings are "site-specific," or designed to be situated in a very particular geographical location. "If buildings are site-specific," Davies writes, "they must be singular, unless sites themselves can be designed and constructed" (2003, 158).

Is Davies's argument persuasive? We first need to determine what "site-specific" means. This might mean that the building plan is tailored precisely to certain constraints of the local site: for example, the building shape might be tailored to fit the unusual slope of the site, or to withstand the local climate, or to match the style of surrounding structures. But if this is what "site-specific" means, it is hard to see why the fact that a building plan is tailored specifically to a unique site would make the building plan singular. Many multiple works of art are tailored to "fit" social conditions in the societies where they are produced: Shakespeare's plays employ Elizabethan dialect, and *Uncle Tom's Cabin* was written to address slavery, for example. But the fact that contemporary instances of these works do not fit contemporary conditions in the same way does not mean they are only copies, and not genuine instances of the works.

However, "site-specific" could also mean something different. Perhaps the idea is not just that the building is tailored to the site, but that the site itself is *a part of* the work. On this view, the designer does not merely plan a building, but rather the entire site. This is perhaps not the usual practice in architecture, but there are some examples: consider Frank Lloyd Wright's famous Fallingwater, which arguably includes not only the house but the waterfall running under it.[22] Without the water, the work seems incomplete (it is called Fallingwater, after all). However, in the case of Fallingwater, it seems that it would not be difficult to find another site with the required features. If we did, it is not clear that refabrication on such a site would produce a mere copy. But is this always the case? Or are there sites that are wholly unique, so that another instantiation of the work is impossible?

One way in which an architectural plan could be singular is for it to refer to the site *as a particular*, rather than in terms of its general features. This might be the case with plans that refer to a site's unique historical properties: for example, a temple built upon the spot where a god or spirit supposedly performed some particular action; a building built upon the site of a unique historical event, such as a battle; or a tomb built to house the body of a specific individual. In these cases, the building plans can only be realized once at any given time because one of the elements of the plan (the site) is truly one of a kind. These cases are exceptional ones in architecture, and in other areas of design they are perhaps rarer still. Yet, here too, perhaps we sometimes find singular designs: consider the 1937 design of the Imperial State Crown for King George VI. One key element of the design was the set of gems embedded in the crown, which were taken from crowns used by previous British monarchs. A refabrication of the design using other gems, even ones with identical chemical composition, would, it seems, only be a copy of the crown.[23] On the whole, then, we should think of design as ontologically more diverse than either music or plastic arts such as painting. While typically multiple, design works can be singular as well.

1.3   Activity, Profession and Practice

In the previous sections, we have worked out a philosophical definition of design. If we return to the examples of design with which we began, such as the iPod and the Eames chair, we can see that they fit the definition nicely. The iPod, for instance, was created to solve a certain set of problems facing portable music players. Our definition can also accommodate other things that we intuitively see as falling under the concept of design, such as architecture and the design of processes, rather than physical objects. In this regard, the definition seems broad enough to fit the concept. However, on reflection we may worry that it is too broad, or covers too much.

For instance, consider industrial engineering: engineers are typically called upon to solve problems by producing new devices that will fulfill a specified set of requirements. On a more mundane level, consider the plumber who has to come up with some new layout of pipes to create a functional plumbing system in a new house. On our definition, both engage in design. This is noted by Bamford, who adds that design, in his sense, can also be found in empirical science. "It is quite appropriate," he writes, "to ask of, say the various trans-Uranian hypotheses formulated by Le Verrier and Adams what they were designed to do. (The answer is that these hypotheses were designed to explain . . .)" (Bamford 1990, 235).

Extending this line of thought, we can also find design, as we have defined it, even farther afield, in realms such as politics and art. The politician who concocts some bold and workable compromise in a delicate piece of legislation is designing, in our sense, as is the screenwriter who comes up with a neat plot twist to resolve some difficulty in her narrative. It seems that the expansiveness of design has reasserted itself. Design may not be everything that we do, as Papanek and some other theorists have thought, but it is, apparently, a part of nearly every sort of activity in which we engage.

However, this conclusion should give us pause. For while the creation of scientific hypotheses, chemical manufacturing processes, plumbing connections, screenplays and constitutions fits our defini-tion of design, these are not products of design in the sense that the Eames chair, Farnsworth House and an online voting system are products of design. We do not call James Madison a great designer, we do not call the theory of evolution by natural selection a great design, and it would be surprising to go to a design show and hear lectures on electrical engineering systems. These facts suggest that our definition of the activity of design is too broad to capture the meaning of the term at play in the central cases with which we began.[24]

One response to this would be to narrow our definition further, so as to exclude these purported cases of design in science, politics and so on. Such a move is suggested by the philosopher Andy Ham-ilton, who endorses the following necessary condition for design: "Designs involve constructions where the visual or sonic appearance or feel is important." As he puts it, "design contains an ineliminable aesthetic component" (Hamilton 2011, 57).[25] On his view, our central examples all count as design because appearance was a key consideration in formulating the plans for them. On the other hand, "changing the chemical composition of a detergent to make it more efficient does not count as design," Hamilton writes, "even if Procter and Gamble describe it so." (57) This condition would clearly rule out some of the problematic cases mentioned above, such as constitutions and scientific hypotheses.

However, Hamilton's proposal does not deal adequately with the full range of problem cases. For one thing, it doesn't exclude artistic cases from our definition, since, in those cases, there typically *is* a concern for "visual or sonic appearance or feel." It is certainly true that much design shares this aesthetic element with art (architecture offers an obvious example). Yet, we intuitively want to place art-works such as the *Mona Lisa* outside the category of design. Hamilton's proposal, however, does not allow us to do this. On the other hand, Hamilton's proposal would apparently exclude from the realm of design the creation of many processes where there is nothing obviously corresponding to the "appearance" of physical products such as iPods and houses. In the design of a new online voting process, for example, "visual or sonic feel" might be a minor or non-existent consideration. Although much design has an aes-thetic aspect, this seems not to be necessary.

But aside from these issues, there is a deeper problem with the entire strategy of trying to narrow our original definition of "design" in the way that Hamilton's approach does. This can best be seen by considering the case of engineering. We would like to set this case apart from our central cases of design. But if we claim that concern with aesthetic appearance is necessary for design, then we are forced to say that when Procter and Gamble describe their chemical research in detergents as "product design," they are using the word in a deviant way. However, this surely isn't the case, as we all under-stand quite well what they mean. "Engineering design" is such a well-entrenched phrase that we should balk at defining our terms in a way that renders it unintelligible.

Hamilton recognizes this point, for he attempts to avoid the conclusion that hidden components such as automobile engines cannot be designed. He says that "the fact that engineers do see the object (even if the rest of us don't) means that it *does* have a minimal aesthetic component, and therefore is designed" (Hamilton 2011, 57; italics added). But the mere fact that engine parts can be seen with the naked eye when made doesn't mean that they are made to provide visual or aesthetic pleasure. Electrical wiring inside walls can be seen as well, at least by the electricians who install it, but how it looks is surely not an "important factor" in how it is struc-tured; indeed, to bring aesthetics into consideration in this context would be strange, and probably even negligent, given the safety issues involved. And in any case, there remain instances, such as the detergent example, where design apparently involves no aesthetic element at all.

Hamilton's approach, then, errs in unduly constricting our con-ception of design.[26] A better approach would be to accept that design, as we defined it in section 1.1, is an activity that plays a role in many different contexts, including engineering. But how then are we to account for the linguistic fact, observed earlier, that Madison, Einstein and your plumber are not called "designers," whereas Eames, Ive and Starck are? Perhaps a solution can be found in another useful suggestion from Bamford, who distinguishes two senses of "design": design as a general sort of "cognitive activity," and design as a "social or institutional practice, or profession" (1990, 233; to keep the two straight, let us follow him in using the upper-case "Design" to refer to the practice or profession and the lower-case "design" to refer to the more generic activity). Drawing this distinction, however, is not enough. We must go on to ask: what makes certain people members of the Design *profession or practice*, as opposed to merely people engaging in the *activity* of design? Until we answer this question, we still lack a substantive understanding of what makes the Eames chair and the iPod different from plumbing systems, constitutions, artworks and the rest.

Before we try to do this, however, we should ask whether Design is a practice or a profession. The difference between the two involves the level of formality and regulation involved. Social practices are simply activities that people engage in, more or less continually, over time, whereas professions involve some sort of formal recognition (Dickie 1984). The law is a profession, since being a lawyer requires formal certification; running or knitting, on the other hand, are merely social practices, since no such certification is required. All professions involve a practice, but not all practices are professions. On this issue, the historian John Heskett observes: "Design . . . has never cohered into a unified profession, such as law, medicine, or architecture, where a license or similar qualification is required to practise, with standards established and protected by self-regulating institutions, and the use of the professional descriptor limited to those who have gained admittance through regulated procedures" (2005, 4; see also Molotch 2003). Perhaps we can say that some specific fields such as graphic design, architecture, have something approximating this structure, but there is no profession "Design" in the sense that there are professions of medicine and law (Bamford 1990). Furthermore, much important Design takes place outside of these professions. For these reasons, it is better to focus on Design as a practice.[27]

How then can we distinguish the practice of Design from the more generic cognitive activity of design? Three features of Design practice seem important here. The first is its practical or utilitarian nature: the Designer creates items that have a practical function. "Practical" here contrasts with "purely theoretical": an item with a practical function is geared to allowing us to change the world, rather than understand it. Scientific hypotheses, in contrast, are explanatory, aiming to allow us to understand the world rather than to alter it. This contrast shouldn't be overstated – scientific hypotheses can have important practical functions as well: they allow us to make vital predictions and to generate useful technologies. Also, Designers often create objects that help us to better understand the world: consider maps, in graphic design, or GPS navigation systems. The real distinction between Design and the empirical sciences is that Design produces items that have the *primary* function of altering the world, rather than explaining it, whereas in the sciences, the primary function is explanation.[28] In the case of the GPS navigation system, for instance, the primary function is navigation, even though this function is achieved by enriching our understanding of geography and spatial layout. The practical focus of the Designer also separates him from the artist mentioned earlier, who designs a solution to his narrative problem. For, despite many differences, the arts and sciences seem to share the primary aim of enriching our understanding of the world, rather than allowing us to change it.[29]

A worry about this insistence on practical function is what it means for areas of design such as interior design or fashion. Can we really describe them as "primarily practical?" It may seem that they are mostly aimed, if not at enhancing understanding, at something else very non-practical, namely aesthetic enjoyment. However, while these fields have a strong aesthetic dimension, they remain primarily practical in the sense that the things they produce are living spaces and clothing. Beautiful rooms that one cannot live in, and beautiful clothes that cannot be worn may succeed as art, but not as Design. So we need not worry that an emphasis on practicality would exclude these areas from Design.

So far we have been able to distinguish Design from natural science and art, but our criterion will hardly help us distinguish Design from engineering. Wiring and plumbing systems are nothing if not practical, yet engineers and plumbers are not, as we have observed, considered Designers.[30] To draw the required distinction here, we need to introduce a second feature of Design practice – a focus on what we might call the "surface" of things. This term is a little misleading, since it suggests a focus only on the visible, exterior shell of an object, as opposed to its interior components. Visible exteriors are obviously one important focus of Design, and in some cases the separation of exterior and interior design is quite sharp, as in contemporary automotive design, where the chassis may be designed by engineers and the body by a distinct Design team. But Design concerns much more than visible exteriors. In some cases, Designers may even produce things that lack anything we might call a "visible exterior," as in the case of designed processes. In our notion of "surface," therefore, we must include more than visual qualities such as shape and color; we must also include what we might call the "interactive dynamics" of the object – the way the object is used and the way it responds to use. In other words, the Designer's point of view on the object is that of the user, and all and only those components or aspects of the object that figure in the user's relation to the object are the province of the Designer.[31] This is in contrast to the perspective of the engineer, who must often focus on elements that, although vital to the object's functioning, do not figure in the user's interaction with it, such as the level of pollution emissions generated by an automobile engine.[32]

To fully capture Design practice's distinctive character, however, we need to re-emphasize one more of its characteristic features. This is the Designer's role as a conceiver of plans, rather than as a builder of objects. We have already noted that design is a conceptual activity that is distinct from building, but in some cases these distinct activities can be carried out by the same person: consider a master furniture maker who designs and then hand-builds custom furniture. Although he designs, as do Designers such as Ive, Starck and Eames, his job, taken as a whole, is quite different from theirs. For the objects created by Ives, Starck and Eames were imagined by them, but not physically constructed by them: they were mass-produced through industrial processes. The difference between the Designer and the furniture maker is not only, or even primarily, one of scale of production, however. An architect might, like a furniture maker, only produce a small number of works during his career. The difference between the architect, and the Designer more generally, and the furniture maker is a difference of method and experience: the furniture maker is involved with the actual construction of his objects in an intimate way in which the typical Designer is not, and indeed cannot, be. Together, these three characteristics give us a picture of Design practice as standing apart from design in general by its focus on conceiving, rather than constructing, the surfaces of primarily practical things.

Having defined Design as this particular kind of practice, we can now say something about its relations to the various professions. In the so-called "Design professions," the practice of Design is the main concern. However, these professionals may do more than Design proper: for example, some may insist on being involved in the design of non-surface features, or on "getting their hands dirty," building prototypes, if not actual instances of their designs. Also, professionals outside the "Design professions" may engage in the practice of Design: engineers may, from inclination or necessity, have to design surface features in the structures they create, and empirical scientists may direct their work toward developing commercial products for everyday use, rather than explaining the natural world. Seeing Design as a practice allows us to better understand its place in the more formalized professional world. In professions such as graphic and industrial design, engaging in this Design practice is the professional's main role, but the practice is also carried on by other professionals, and even by people working outside of any institutionalized profession at all.

1.4   The Rise of the Designer

Having identified the practice that we call "Design," we can now raise a further question: where did it come from? Some of the other professions we have mentioned in the course of our discussion – politics, science and so on – are very old, dating in some recognizable form back to antiquity. Design, however, is different – it is a quintessentially modern phenomenon. Historians differ as to the date of its exact origins, but generally its beginnings are thought to lie in the early industrial revolution. As one writer puts it, "design historians have tended to regard processes of industrialization as significant for providing the conditions necessary for the emergence of a distinct practice of design" (Lees-Maffei 2010, 13).

To appreciate Design's origins, and some of the important conceptual problems arising from them, it is crucial to view the Designer in contrast with another figure whom he largely supplanted – the craftsperson. We must be careful here, since "craft" is another slippery word with several distinct meanings, some of which very much overlap with "art" and "design" (Greenhalgh 1997; Shiner 2012). The contrast we need to draw involves one quite narrow and very old sense of craft, which we might call "tradition-based craft." This includes things such as the hand-making of furniture, tools, pottery or buildings according to traditional methods and forms. In tradition-based crafts, the focus is not on novelty, but on following established criteria and rules that the craftsperson learns from a master. The craftsperson creates things, but does not design them: he inherits a set of standardized forms that have evolved over time, through centuries of trial and error and subtle modification. The key factor in tradition-based craft is not creativity, but skill in applying the established rules, something that can take many years to perfect.[33]

A widespread breakdown of the tradition-based craft system of production began when the industrial revolution introduced methods of mass production and the division and specialization of labor in the seventeenth and eighteenth centuries. The change was not primarily one of technology, but of organization, as in Josiah Wedgwood's reorganization of his pottery factories in the early eighteenth century (Forty [1986] 2005). Whereas in the past a single skilled potter cast each entire pot, now the task was divided into discrete phases, each allotted to a different worker. One of these was a Designer: Wedgwood hired artists to create the patterns and forms for his different lines of pottery. Although the Designer conceived each type of ceramic ware, he was not involved in making any of the pots, but only in sketching and drawing patterns for them. His role, however, was more critical than that of any other worker, for only he considered the item to be produced as a whole. As mass production and the division of labor spread, this model was applied to a wide range of goods.

This general account of the origins of Design needs some qualification, however. In a sense, the modern Designer who emerges in the industrial revolution has some earlier precursors in ancient professions such as architecture and ship building (Jones 1970, 21). The scale and complexity of large vessels, for example, meant that a single person could not build them, and, further, that one person had to oversee plans for the whole to ensure a cogent design.

However, although some ships no doubt required new plans and modifications, shipwrights could draw upon a repertoire of traditional forms. It is more clearly in architecture where the Designer first emerges, since the need for a new type of building would be more common than needs for new types of vessels. We should bear in mind, however, that even ancient architecture does not correspond entirely to Design in its modern form. Ancient architects were also engineers (the most famous ancient treatise on architecture, Vitruvius' *Ten Books of Architecture*, contains discussions of water cisterns and siege machines), and cases of anything like mass production were perhaps rare. Nonetheless, the fact that architecture is the earliest manifestation of the practice of Design does much to explain the oft-noted fact that architecture, despite being somewhat anomalous in not typically involving mass production, has held a central place in thinking about Design (Sparke 2004, 58).

In any event, for most of history, architecture was exceptional. Prior to industrialization, the production of most goods was carried out, without any figure corresponding to the Designer, by tradition-based craft. The origin of the modern Design professions, with the advent of industrialization, thus represents a kind of rupture with previous ways of making. It represents a massive shift of responsibility from the traditional, collective behavior of the society to the shoulders of the Designer. The profound economic and social implications of this shift have been recognized since the origins of the practice: as long as Design has been around, it has been the subject of acute social anxieties. Governments and businessmen have worried about the impact of declining standards of Design on export trade, and educators have fretted about how to instruct and foster the Designers of the future. In nineteenth-century Britain, for example, no fewer than three parliamentary committees were struck to investigate the state of British Design and to make recommendations for its improvement (Forty [1986] 2005, 58–61). As well, influential cultural figures, such as William Morris and John Ruskin in the nineteenth century, have worried about the broader cultural consequences of our increasing dependence on Design and mass production. As our culture has become more characterized by consumerism, these anxieties have only intensified. As one Designer put it, "design . . . has become of more pressing importance than ever before: simply because there is a greater quantity of it and fewer people ever escape from the sight of it" (Pye 1978, 91). A twentieth-century Designer may not have been exaggerating too much when he pronounced, "Design controls our whole life – our whole happiness depends upon it" (Grillo 1960, 15). In the next chapter, we turn to the manner in which the Designer undertakes this heroic task, and examine more closely the process of Design.

2

The Design Process

In the previous chapter, we saw that, in modern society, the Designer has an important and quite daunting role. Given this, there has been much interest, and more than a little anxiety, over how he goes about this task. In this chapter, we examine some philosophical questions concerning the creative process of the Designer. What is the method by which he achieves his results? How should he be trained so as to best prepare him for the job? Is there something inherently mysterious or ineffable about the Design process?

2.1 The Challenges of Design

In order to consider the process employed by Designers, we must try to bring into better focus the general sort of problem that they face. So far we have said that the Designer attempts to create plans for the surface features of a novel device or process that will solve some primarily practical problem. But just what sort of problem is this?

At the most basic level, the "practical" aspect of a Design problem can usually be viewed as a problem of function or utility.[1] There is some task that we want performed – brewing a pot of coffee, say – and the Designer's job is to create an object that performs it well. Such functional requirements are typically specified in a design brief: a specification of requirements that the Designer's plans must satisfy, provided by her client (for some examples, see Cross 2011). The brief, however, will typically pose challenges beyond simply creating an object with a specified function, for it will specify constraints on how the function can be satisfied. It may specify a maximum unit cost of production for the object, for example, or specify the use of certain materials. It may also introduce other constraints, such as requirements for stylistic or functional compatibility with other products produced by the company, or safety requirements mandated by laws and product codes.[2]

These economic and legal aspects of the Designer's task are, of course, entangled with the functional aspect, since they will prohibit many functional solutions that would otherwise be desirable (Pye 1978). But they are also entangled with aspects of the Design challenge that extend beyond functionality. One of the most noted and significant trends in Design during the past century has been the increasing importance of aspects of the object apart from its practical functionality, such as its aesthetic appeal, its style and its expressive qualities (Postrel 2003). It is one thing for a coffee-making device to brew a pot of coffee effectively, but another thing for it to be beautiful or elegantly stylish, or for it to capture the imagination by expressing a particular lifestyle. These latter features, however, are often crucial elements of Design success. As one writer nicely puts it, for many products, "the object is not the object" (Hine 1986, 66). Cultivating these more abstract aesthetic and symbolic qualities in the Design product can be a major part of the Designer's challenge.[3]

These considerations are perhaps enough to show the potential complexity of the problem facing the Designer in the form of the design brief. But there is also a more philosophical line of thought suggesting that the Designer's problem is greater still. This line of thought is essentially that the artefacts produced by Design not only serve functional, symbolic and aesthetic aims, but also play a more fundamental role in influencing human life. The basic idea here is that, in the words of the philosopher Peter Paul Verbeek, these artefacts play a "mediating role," whereby they "shape a relation between human beings and the world" (2005, 208).

This line of thought has several sources. One is philosophical reflection on the impact of technology. In the early and mid twentieth century, many writers expressed anxiety about the radical changes that were being produced by new but increasingly pervasive technologies, such as television and nuclear weapons. These thinkers explored the ways in which the replacement of older practices and ways of living with new ones made possible by technology was altering how people thought and behaved (see, for example, Mumford 1934; Borgmann 1984; and Winner 1980). Although these studies tended to focus on "high-tech" innovations, they led naturally to a greater appreciation for how all material artefacts, from high-tech devices down to more everyday artefacts produced by Design, influence human life and thought. Consider, for example, the humble dining table (Verbeek 2005, 207). The design of a dining table might seem to be a mere aesthetic choice, but this is not quite so. At a rectangular table, someone (traditionally the "man of the house") sits at the "head position," whereas at a round table, everyone has an equal position. The effect is subtle, something that the people involved may not even be aware of, but differences of hierarchy and status are often shaped and maintained by just such subtle influences.

Awareness of such effects has been reinforced by many studies in the history of Design, which have documented the subtle but often profound ways in which humble objects such as furniture can deeply influence the way we act and think (Lees-Maffei and Houze 2010). Adrian Forty's analysis of changes in the twentieth-century office desk is a case in point. In the nineteenth century, office clerks typically worked at high-backed or roll-top desks with numerous drawers and pigeon holes for papers. Such desks gave the clerk a certain amount of privacy from prying managerial eyes, and certain degree of control over his own paperwork. As Forty put it, "such a desk encapsulates the responsibility, trust and status given to some clerks" ([1986] 2005, 124–5). Twentieth-century office redesign saw such desks eliminated in favor of austere flat-top desks with little or no drawer or storage space. This apparently simple Design change had a profound effect on human relations in the office, dramatically eroding the traditional autonomy of the individual clerk.

Finally, within the profession of Design itself, there has long been an appreciation by Designers of the interconnectedness of the problems they face with broader social, ethical and political problems. These connections were clearly manifested in cases like the automobile, where innovations that made cars widely desired objects had massive ramifications on social patterns of settlement and work, environmental problems such as increased air pollution, and even romantic and sexual practices (Harris 2001).

The prominent American Designer Buckminster Fuller expressed this interconnectedness in his notion of "comprehensive designing," according to which the tackling of any given Design problem must take into account the various other problems connected with it (see also Jones 1970).

When the Designer's task is conceived of in this comprehensive way, he naturally becomes the focus of great, even messianic, hopes. He emerges as the "change-master" of modern life (Heskett 2005, 20), a figure with "the power to continuously remodel the whole fabric of industrial society from top to bottom" (Jones 1970, 32). On the other hand, the task facing the Designer can seem so daunting as to be hopeless. The Designer, viewed in this more pessimistic mood, stands in a stark contrast with his forebear, the tradition-based craftsperson. The craftsperson's challenge was to develop the skill required to produce the forms developed and perfected by the hundreds of years of tradition that preceded him. As anyone who has tried to cultivate such skill knows, this is a formidable enough challenge. But it pales in comparison with the task of the Designer, which is nothing less than to reshape the way people think, act and see the world. Christopher Alexander captured this predicament rather poetically in his description of the modern Designer, sundered from a craft tradition: "bewildered, the form-maker stands alone" (1964, 4).

Before we consider how the Designer might respond to this formidable challenge, we should examine the possibility that we have greatly exaggerated the situation facing the Designer. One might agree that Design has the potential to reshape society in profound ways, but still maintain that this is not really the Designer's concern. The Designer, it might be said, should not concern herself with these larger problems, or try to engage in "comprehensive designing." Rather, she should merely "stick to the brief." These larger issues are the proper concern, not of Designers, but of someone else – perhaps the companies who decide which sorts of designs to commission or put into production, or perhaps the politicians whose job it is to regulate the use of certain products. In support of the idea of "sticking to the brief," we can offer at least one important consideration, which is that Designers who don't stick to the brief, and who allow larger concerns about political or ethical issues to come into play, are liable to be fired by their employers for insubordination.

It is true, of course, that Designers, like other professionals, are significantly constrained by the economic system in which they work – they are not free to reshape the world at their whim, but must satisfy their corporate masters. However, it is also true that those corporate masters are increasingly being enticed or compelled to bring broader considerations into play, as can be seen in the dramatic increase in the role of environmental issues as a factor in commercial Design, and in the growth of increasing product options to meet diverse consumer demands (Postrel 2003).[4] Furthermore, even when Designers are compelled to ignore certain aspects of their problem, this hardly means that those aspects disappear. If these aspects of the Design problem are to be dealt with by captains of industry or politicians, they must deal with them (if they deal with them at all), ultimately, by introducing them into the brief they give to some other Designer. Therefore, even if considering the Design problem in its full scope seems idealistic, and somewhat out of line with the day-to-day work of most Designers, it is still of the first importance in a consideration of the Design professions in general.

2.2   A Crisis of Confidence

Our sketch of the Designer's task makes it appear daunting in light of the number of different levels involved. In addition to the practical aspect, the Designer apparently has to consider the functional, the symbolic, the aesthetic, the mediating, and even the social and political dimensions of the project. At any given level of the Design problem, the range of possibilities can be very great. Incompatibilities between various options at different levels further complicate the situation: for example, materials that would satisfy functional requirements may have the wrong symbolic connotations. Commenting on this situation, the Design theorist Christopher Alexander wrote in the mid-1960s that "today more and more design problems are reaching insoluble levels of complexity" (1964, 3).

But beyond this complexity, there is a still more fundamental difficulty lurking in the Design problem. This is what the Design theorist Christopher Jones called the "instability of the problem." Frequently, he observes, "the act of tracing out the intermediate steps [in the solution of a Design problem] exposes unforeseen difficulties or suggests better objectives," with the result that "the pattern of the original problem may change so drastically that the designers are thrown back to square one" (1970, 10). Design would be difficult enough if the aims were fixed, but in fact the overall aims themselves can shift in light of progress, or lack thereof. Many theorists have remarked on this feature of Design: Donald Schön, for instance, discusses the need for Designers to "frame" the situations they confront in such a way that certain goals, and possibilities for attaining them, come into focus. At certain points in the Design process, he observes, Designers may need to "re-frame" the situation, focusing on a different problem and bringing different aims into play (1983, 40–2).[5]

All of this complexity in Design problems naturally heightens anxieties about the very foundations of Design practice (Alexander 1964; Jones 1965; Schön 1983; Simon 1996). How is it that the Designer can solve such problems? A traditional answer to this question is that good Designers simply have a knack of coming up with something that "does the trick," just as good artists have a knack of creating beautiful or intriguing artworks. Good Designers, in other words, can rely on *intuition* to guide them (Molotch 2003, 31).

However, when one takes into account the full scope of the Design problem, this answer seems rather unsatisfactory. Can the Designer really rely on "intuition" to sort this all out? This worry is intensified by the nature of the mass-production system in which Design is typically embedded, where Design decisions can have immense impacts on the fortunes of a company or product, or even of an entire nation competing in the global marketplace. How can we be sure, it is asked, that our Designers are being trained in the right way, so as to be prepared to meet the challenges of their profession? To say that Designers must have intuition, a mysterious quality that cannot be assessed or understood, leaves us apparently powerless to improve our education system with the aim of producing better Designers.

Such worries about the capacity and integrity of Design practice have produced a number of responses. One was the rise, in the 1960s, of the so-called "Design Methods" or "Design Science" movement. The basic premise behind the movement was the notion that, in Alexander's words, "the intuitive resolution of contemporary design problems simply lies beyond a single individual's integrative grasp" (1964, 5). A new account of the Design process was therefore needed, an account that would demonstrate its ability to effectively tackle Design problems. Such an account would also strengthen public confidence in the Designer: Design would become open, transparent and assessable. As the economist Herbert Simon put it, there would no longer be any possibility of "the design process hiding behind the cloak of 'judgment' or 'experience'" (Simon 1996, 135).

Simon, who was one of the leading figures associated with this movement, argued that the reliance on intuition had led to a marginalization of Design within the contemporary university. In the university setting, Simon argued, the highest prestige accrues to the pure sciences, due to their much vaunted "scientific method," widely viewed as a paradigm of objectivity and rationality, and the key to material progress. Situated next to the pure sciences, Design, with its intuitive and "cook-booky" methodology, looked flimsy and amateurish. The result, Simon claimed, was that academic departments that ought to be doing Design were instead doing pure science, such as materials research. The problem was thus not just an erosion of Design's prestige, but an erosion of the very discipline itself. The way to halt it, he held, was to articulate "a science of design, a body of intellectually tough, analytic, partly formalizable, partly empirical, teachable doctrine about the design process."[6]

Many early works in Design Methods tended to be, in line with Simon's vision, highly formalized and mathematical in nature (see, for example, Alexander 1964; Gregory 1966; and Jones 1970). These attracted much subsequent criticism for being overly "scientific," and some of the leading figures of the movement later distanced themselves from their earlier efforts (Alexander 1971; Jones 1977). However, investigation into the nature of the Design process did not stop, but continued in both theoretical and empirical studies of how Designers work and think (for a review, see Bayazit 2004). The key idea underpinning this work was articulated by Bruce Archer, who claimed: "There exists a designerly way of thinking and communicating that is both different from scientific and scholarly ways of thinking and communicating, and as powerful . . . when applied to its own kind of problems" (Archer 1979, 17). Following up on this idea, Design theorists have continued to identify and characterize the various techniques and strategies that are appropriate for Designers to use in solving actual problems (for a review of this work, see Cross 2011).

2.3 The Epistemological Problem

In thinking about the difficulty of Design problems, and the attempts to formulate a Design methodology that it has inspired, it will help us to get clearer about what the fundamental difficulty really is. This difficulty is not a problem of scale, due to the complexity of the Design problem. Nor is it a difficulty concerning the somewhat unstable nature of the Design problem itself. Rather, the fundamental problem for the Design process is an *epistemological* problem, a problem concerning the sort of knowledge that good Designers apparently require.

To see this problem, we must first ask: What makes someone a good Designer? One might answer that a good Designer is simply someone who comes up with good Designs: effective solutions to Design problems. But while this may be necessary for being a good Designer, it isn't sufficient. Design is not merely the act of producing a solution to a problem: rather, it is essential that the problem guide the formulation of the solution in some rational way. A person who was extraordinarily lucky and happened to bang out several fantastic Designs by accident would not be a great Designer – he would merely be extraordinarily lucky. Another way to phrase our requirement, drawing on our earlier discussion of rational Design in section 1.1, is this: a good Designer has a justified belief that, given the nature of the problem and the solution he proposes, his solution will work. Note that it is not enough that the Designer *believes* that his plan will work: blind self-confidence will not make you a good Designer any more than blind luck will. The Designer's confidence must be *justified*: he must have some evidence or reasons to support it.[7]

The requirement for justification should not be over-stated, for Designers will almost never have, and surely do not need, *conclusive* evidence that their Design will succeed. Design inherently involves, we can admit, a degree of risk. But if success is always to a degree uncertain, one can still have reasonable confidence of success, and it is on the possibility of even this degree of confidence that we must focus. The epistemological difficulty for Design is, in Galle's words: "How . . . could the designer know (or be confident) at that time that the artifact would eventually serve its purpose?" (2011, 94). If we cannot answer this question, it seems that we cannot say that there are good Designers.[8]

We can best appreciate why this problem arises for Design by first seeing why it fails to arise for two other kinds of production: tradition-based craft and contemporary art. Consider first the case of tradition-based craft. What reason does a tradition-based craftsperson have for believing that what he makes – his table, or wagon, for example – will be successful, that it will work? The first thing to see is that this question – will it work? – is an empirical question, or a question concerning a matter of fact. This is clear insofar as we focus just on the aim of functionality. To know whether a given sort of table, for example, is going to function well, we have to subject it to use and see what happens. But the empirical nature of the question remains when we extend its scope to the other aspects of the Design problem: its symbolic, aesthetic or mediating aspects, for example. Along these various dimensions, will it be successful or not? We can speculate, of course, that it will or it won't, but without actually observing how it impacts people, we cannot really say one way or the other. So if the tradition-based craftsperson has a reason for believing that his product will work, then it seems that he must have some empirical knowledge concerning the object's behavior.

Indeed, it is plausible to think that he has such knowledge. The craftsperson's reason for believing that his product will "work" is something that, along with his repertoire of forms and techniques, he inherits from his craft tradition: the item is the result of a long process of trial and error, during which minor alterations in the form have been made in response to problems, and tested by experience.[9] Another way to look at it is that the craftsperson has the knowledge in question because his process, though heavily dependent upon skill, is not really a creative one, but involves the skilful reproduction of an established type that has already been tested and is known to have been adequately successful.

In the case of Design, however, this is not so, for the Designer's process *is* creative, generating a *new* entity or process. As in the case of the craftsperson, a good Designer must be justified in thinking that his product will work. But given that it is novel, and has not been subjected to trial-and-error testing by tradition, the Designer seems to be left with no reason for confidence in its ability to satisfy the aims for which it was created. It is, as it were, a shot in the dark. Of course, the Designer can speculate that it will work well, but such speculation amounts only to *belief* that it will work well, not to *justified belief* that it will work well.[10]

We can bring out the epistemological problem inherent in Design in a slightly different way by contrasting it with a second mode of production in which it fails to arise: the fine arts. As mentioned, Design differs from tradition-based crafts in being a creative mode of production. In this, Design has a close affinity with the fine arts, which place a heavy emphasis upon creativity and originality (as mentioned earlier, some of the first Designers literally were artists, such as the painters whom Wedgwood recruited to create patterns for his ceramic wares). On at least some ways of thinking about art, however, fine artists do not face the Designer's epistemological difficulty.

To see this, consider one common way of thinking about art. This view takes the artist's aim to be producing a work that expresses something within himself: either a feeling or an emotional state, or an idea or point of view – something that the artist "has to say." As an example of the first view, we may take R. G. Collingwood's theory of art as expression, on which the artist creates the work as a means of working out the particular nature of an unclear emotional state he is feeling (Collingwood 1938). A prominent example of the second view is Arthur Danto's theory of art, according to which the artist creates a work that takes on a particular sort of symbolic meaning, in the context of art history and theory (Danto 1981). In either sort of theory, the artist produces a vehicle for a feeling or an idea. Because this feeling or idea comes from within himself, he is able to guide the creative process so that the product embodies the emotion or the meaning he has in mind. Of course, this doesn't mean that producing fine art is easy, or always successful (there is much bad art). But, given this general description, we can at least see how it is possible.[11]

This possibility, however, hinges on the fact that the product is a vehicle for something to which the artist has access within himself. Since he has immediate access to his own emotions or ideas through introspection, he can, as it were, know a priori, or independently of experience, when his creation succeeds in expressing it. But in the case of Design, this sort of a priori knowledge is not possible, since the Designer's aim is not merely to express something within himself, but to create something that will function adequately in the world. And whether a novel entity will function adequately in the world is not something we can know a priori. The Designer can imagine ways of realizing his aim, but, unlike the artist, he has within himself no means for confirming that they will be successful. He *would* have a way to confirm this, had he access to the craftperson's tradition of an established type, but of course his lack of access to such a tradition is part of what makes him a Designer.

The comparison between contemporary art and Design can perhaps be illuminated in a different way by considering an earlier notion of art. In ancient Greece, the epic poetry of Homer played a central cultural role. One aspect of this role was Homeric poetry's supposed connection to knowledge (Irwin 1989). The Greeks thought that Homer's poems were not only a source of pleasure, or a source of history, but also a source of genuine knowledge on many topics, including practical matters such as military strategy and chariot driving, as well as more theoretical subjects, such as morality and politics. It is difficult for us to conceive of poetry in this way, given that we have come to view the sciences and philosophy, broadly conceived, as playing these roles, and poetry as chiefly concerned with personal expression. But in ancient Greece, the view that Homeric poetry was a source of wisdom was well entrenched.

It was not uncontested, however; it was famously attacked by the philosopher Plato in his book *The Republic*. Plato begins by noting that the poet's skill lies not in making actual things but in making images, or imitations, of them. He does not create the actual words of Achilles, but only an imitation of them; he does not create an actual good man, but an imitation of one. If it is true, then, that the poet's works convey knowledge, they must contain true images or faithful imitations of what they depict. But, Plato asks, how would the poet be capable of rendering such true images or representations? Creating imitations in itself does not require any knowledge of that that is imitated. Plato asks, "Does an imitator have knowledge of whether the things he makes are fine or right through having made use of them?" He does not; neither does he know this from asking those who might possess knowledge about the actual things themselves. The conclusion is that "an imitator has no worthwhile knowledge of the things he imitates" (602a–b).[12]

The modern Designer, it seems, is in a somewhat similar difficulty. The Designer does not make mere imitations, as the poet does; she creates actual things. But the Designer is dogged by an epistemological worry analogous to that faced by the poet: how does he know that the thing he produces will work? In the case of poetry, we might say that the problem is generated by a mismatch between method and aim. The method of poetry, which involves the construction of imitations or images, does not line up with the aim attributed to it by popular Greek culture: conveying knowledge of how the world is. We can analyze Design, in similar terms, as a hybrid of two mismatched elements: the aims of tradition-based craft and a method unsuited to attaining them.

Greek thought did have a way of resolving Plato's difficulty concerning Homer's poetry, which was to appeal to a special, inexplicable ability possessed by the poet. In Greek culture, for example, the poets were commonly thought to receive their wisdom directly from the gods, via inspiration. Whereas Plato portrays epic poetry in the *Republic* as a misconceived sort of technique, on this view poetry is not a technique at all, but a kind of divine power conferred on certain lucky mortals by the gods.[13] In the case of Design, one can resolve the epistemological difficulty in much the same way, as we have seen earlier, by attributing to the Designer a special "intuition" for discerning the necessary solution to a given problem. However, such solutions do not dispel, but only rename, the problem at issue. In his day, Plato insisted that appeals to divine inspiration were no longer enough to justify the poet's claim to a position of social authority and prestige. In our own time, appeals to "Designer's intuition" seem to ring hollow in a similar way.

2.4   Are Design Problems Ill-Defined?

The premise underlying our epistemological problem is that Design problems are, although complex and difficult, genuine problems that call for a rational approach. The epistemological problem is to figure out how such a rational approach could be available to the Designer. Before we examine some possible solutions to this problem, we must consider one alternative view which rejects the problem, and the premise on which it is based. Rather than trying to explain how a good Designer can rationally approach Design problems, this approach argues that there really are no such problems in the first place.

One source for this view is the influential paper "Dilemmas in a general theory of planning" by the Design theorists Horst Rittel and Melvin Webber (1973). In this paper, Rittel and Webber are mainly concerned with what they call "policy problems," or "problems of societal systems," such as the setting of state school curricula, tax policy and government strategies to address crime and poverty. But their discussion also extends to more traditional Design problems, such as the design of public infrastructure, like subways and freeways. Also, as will be discussed below, their views are frequently extended further to apply to the Design of smaller-scale goods and processes, and Design problems in general.

Rittel and Webber argue that planning problems are of a particularly vexing kind: they are, as they put it, "wicked problems." The term, as they acknowledge, is a little misleading: their idea is not that these problems concern anything evil, but that the problems themselves are tricky, hard to handle and somewhat deceptive in their nature. They contrast wicked problems with what they call "tame problems," which are "well behaved," and which can be tackled and solved by rational approaches. As examples of tame problems, Rittel and Webber offer chess problems, such as achieving checkmate in five moves from a given position, and problems of applied science, such as analyzing the chemical structure of a particular substance.

Why are planning problems "wicked problems"? Rittel and Webber identify ten features of wicked problems, features that make them particularly intractable to rational solution. Some of these features point toward the epistemological problem that we discussed earlier. For example, they note that, in many cases, testing potential solutions to a planning problem is hard or impossible: planners are often unable to carry out adequate trial-and-error tests of their plans, for example. They also observe that each planning problem is unique, making it hard to see how a planner could develop the expertise needed to address new cases. These features, as we've seen, are a part of what makes Design problems epistemologically problematic. But Rittel and Webber's notion of the wicked problem goes beyond these factors to posit a more fundamental difficulty: for wicked problems, they claim, "the problem can't be defined until the solution has been found."

They illustrate using the example of strategies for solving "the poverty problem." What exactly *is* the poverty problem? They write:

> Does poverty mean low income? Yes, in part. But what are the determinants of low income? Is it deficiency of the national and regional economies, or is it deficiencies of cognitive and occupational skills within the labor force? . . . or does the poverty problem reside in deficient physical and mental health? . . . Does it include cultural deprivation? Spatial dislocation? Problems of ego identity? Deficient political and social skills – and so on. If we can formulate the problem by tracing it to some sort of sources . . . then we have thereby also formulated a solution. (1973, 161)

Rittel and Webber make two points here. The first is that the phrase "the poverty problem" is ill defined, or ambiguous: the phrase can be taken to refer to any number of distinct situations – low income, lack of political influence, lack of access to culture, and so forth. Their second point is that each of these particular problems, taken on its own, is easy to solve – in fact, once recognized, the problem *is* solved: "If we recognize deficient mental health services as part of the problem," they write, "then – trivially enough – 'improvement of mental health services' is a specification of solution [*sic*]" (161).

In a sense, then, for Rittel and Webber, solutions to planning problems are really not difficult to find at all; they materialize trivially once the problem has been interpreted. The challenge of planning resides entirely in deciding how to interpret the problem in the first place. But how to interpret the problem is a political choice, not a technical problem, since there is really no such thing as *the* problem. It is therefore also a choice to which the planner brings no special expertise. "Planning," they write, "is a component of politics." This has profound implications for how we conceive of the role of the planner, as Rittel suggests elsewhere when he states, "The planner is not an expert" (Protzen and Harris 2010, 161). It also has implications for how planning is carried out. "The role of the planner," he writes, "is that of a midwife or teacher rather than one who plans for others. Instead he shows others how to plan for themselves" (146).

The rather dramatic consequences of this perspective make it important to determine the extent to which the notion of the "wicked problem" can be extended to Design problems in general. It is sometimes asserted that "design problems in general are examples of what Rittel and Webber called 'wicked problems'" (Vincente et al. 1997; Cross 2011, 147) or that, in Design, "wickedness is the norm" (Coyne 2005; see also Buchanan 1992). On this view, it is not only large-scale problems of public policy, such as the ones discussed by Rittel and Webber, that are wicked or ill defined, but all Design problems, down to mundane examples like laying out a factory control room, or designing a new piece of furniture. But is this really so? What reasons can be given for thinking that *all* Design problems are ill defined?

One consideration that can be put forward is the fact that Designers' clients themselves often do not seem to really know what they want. The client may provide the Designers with a brief specifying certain requirements and aims, but the brief may be sketchy and refer to very generic desiderata, such as "greater efficiency," or "an exciting new look." Further, clients will often ignore the brief requirements altogether when given a plan aimed at other goals that happen to catch their interest (much to the chagrin of those Designers who "stick to the brief"). This suggests that no definite problem existed to begin with.

However, this behavior on the part of the client needs careful examination. Say, for the sake of argument, that the client does have a very specific aim in mind for a project: increasing driver comfort in an economy car, for example. Even if this were the case, we would still expect, of course, that the client will not know *exactly* what he wants, since what he wants exactly is a solution to his problem, and if he already had the solution then he wouldn't be hiring a Designer in the first place. So some unclarity on the client's part does not entail that there is no genuine problem. A more important point, however, is that the fact that Design problems can be changed midway through an attempt at solution – what we earlier called the "instability of Design problems" – does not entail that the problem was ill defined in the first place. Say again that the initial problem that the client meant to solve was improving driver comfort. During the Design process, the client or the Designer could decide, for all sorts of reasons, to drop this particular problem in favor of another one. This wouldn't entail that the original problem was ill defined, nor that rational methods were not applicable in trying to solve it. To see this, we can note that a similar kind of shift happens in natural science all the time: a scientist starts out attempting to explain one phenomena, but switches to another problem that seems, given the circumstances, easier to solve or more interesting than the original.

It seems, then, that we do not have a compelling reason to extend Rittel and Webber's notion of the wicked problem to Design problems in general: Design problems are not always ill-defined problems. Of course, sometimes they are, and a prudent Designer will be wary of this possibility. When a Designer is called upon to create, for example, a "more efficient office," they should ask what exactly "efficiency" means. But dealing with wicked problems is only one part of the Design process. Indeed, even when dealing with wicked problems, there is still more to the Design process than described by Rittel and Webber. For, contrary to what they say, when the ambiguity in a wicked problem is eliminated, the problem is hardly solved. To take their example, they write that once we see poverty as involving mental health, "'improvement of mental health services' is a specification of solution" (1973, 161). But this hardly counts as a "specification of solution," since "improve mental health services" is far from being a "plan" one can see as likely to succeed: this is an aim, not a plan.

In sum, the difficulty of Design cannot be attributed entirely to the ambiguity of the problems it addresses: Designers do confront genuine problems that call for a rational approach. However, this takes us right back to our epistemological problem: how is such an approach possible?

2.5 Some Responses

How might we respond to the epistemological problem at the heart of the Design process? One radical response would be to reject the practice of Design altogether and instead return to some version of the system of production embodied in tradition-based craft. Something like this response is perhaps discernible in views that reject contemporary architecture and endorse instead the reimplementation of traditional and "time-tested" architectural patterns. Roger Scruton, for example, writes: "The failure of modernism, in my view, lies not in the fact that it has produced no great or beautiful buildings . . . It lies in the absence of any reliable patterns or types" (2011, 317).

Scruton grants that contemporary architecture has had its successes, but his call for a return to tradition is premised on the idea that, on the whole, it has been a failure (see Scruton 1979, 1994). But this, it could be argued, is unduly cynical. While there is bad Design, including bad architecture, there is also much that is good. The epistemological problem should therefore move us not to reject Design, but rather to try to explain how it manages to be as successful as it is.

One way to do this might be to argue as follows. Some Designers just seem able to examine a problem and come up with ideas that "work." But this is not surprising, since creativity is inherently a somewhat mysterious capacity. There are many other professions in which some people are more creative than others, and who knows how they get their ideas? Perhaps psychology will eventually succeed in determining why certain people are more creative than others, and when they do we will have a better handle on what makes for a great Designer. But, given that creativity is still relatively poorly understood, we should not be ashamed to say that some people simply have the "gift" of being great at Design, any more than we are ashamed to say that some people simply have the gift of being better at having mathematical insights, or writing poetry.

There is no doubt that creativity is centrally important to the Design process. However, it is important to re-emphasize that the problem at issue is not really a problem about creativity, but about *knowledge*. Creativity is the capacity to come up with ideas that are novel, unanticipated or unforeseen. To think creatively is to think differently. But the problem that we have identified is not: how can the Designer come with ideas that are novel or different? Rather, it is: how can the Designer come up with ideas that are *likely to solve a Design problem*?[14] Another way to put the point is that even if we had a full understanding of why certain individuals are able to formulate very creative Design concepts, we would still need to explain how they can have confidence that those Design concepts will actually solve the problems they address, when they apparently lack the kind of empirical knowledge that such confidence requires.

A second response would be to insist that we have fundamentally mischaracterized the nature of the Designer's activity. The Designer's job, it might be said, is not to provide a corroborated solution to the problem, in which he can be confident, so much as to provide a *proposal* for a solution. We might take the plan offered by the Designer as being analogous to a hypothesis formulated by a scientist to explain certain natural phenomena.[15] To offer a hypothesis, a scientist need not have proof that it is true, or even likely to be true. Philosophers make this point by drawing a distinction, within science, between the *context of discovery* and the *context of justification*. In the context of justification, when scientists are assessing their hypotheses in terms of their likely truth, supporting evidence is needed. But the *formulating* of hypotheses occurs in a different context, and need not be guided by supporting evidence or even any rational process at all (a scientist might come up with a new hypothesis in a dream, for example). Similarly, to offer a solution to a Design problem, the Designer need not have proof that it will work. Of course, we will ultimately want to test the Design to make sure that it does work, just as we want to test a scientific hypothesis to see if it is true. But it isn't the Designer's responsibility to do this testing, and so good Designers do not require the sort of knowledge we have described.

In line with this, it is of course true that much product testing on new Design prototypes is carried out by corporations before they actually go into mass production. This kind of testing, coupled with market research, is often an important part of the manufacturing process, and is closely linked to Design practice. In the case of products with legal safety requirements, this kind of "in-house" testing may be a necessity, and may be related to legal product specifications. Granted, there are certain aspects of the Design problem that are more difficult to test in this way, including qualitative aspects such as comfort or aesthetic appeal (Alexander 1964, 98). However, in principle, it would be possible to at least gather a sample of responses to these aspects of a new Design. This aspect of Design is often reflected in formal theoretical models of the Design process, which typically include stages like "analysis" and "evaluation" (e.g., the "Function-Behaviour-Structure" model of Gero and Kannengiesser 2004; for discussion, see Dorst and Vermaas 2005).[16]

In reality, however, this kind of in-house product testing may be very limited; in some cases, there may be very little testing done prior to production at all (Molotch 2003, 45–7). But we might reply that, even in these cases, products are still tested, albeit *after* production, in the marketplace. After all, many products go into production only to quickly disappear because of some inadequacy in the Design. Whomever we see as doing the "testing," the key point is that it isn't the Designer. Designers have an obligation only to come up with designs, not to justify the efficacy of those designs.

This line of thinking yields a Darwinian view of Design, according to which Designers merely propose various novel entities or processes, some of which "survive" and some of which "die." This analogy, however, highlights exactly what is problematic about this line of thought as a response to our problem. In the case of Darwinian evolution by natural selection in natural species, the mutations that are acted upon by selective forces are generated at random. They need not be "good guesses" at a solution to an adaptive problem: all that matters, for evolution to occur, is that there are a sufficient number and variety of them. But Design is not like that: Design is not about generating vast numbers of randomly produced forms and putting them into testing and production. Obviously, this would be prohibitively expensive and gratuitously wasteful of the Designer's expertise. Rather, Designers, unlike chromosomes, *do* strive to produce "good guesses," and good Designers often succeed (Rittel and Webber 1973). But then we are right back to our original problem – how is it that a Designer can make these "good guesses?"[17]

One suggestion might be to consider again the case of scientific hypotheses. As mentioned above, scientific hypotheses are formulated in a context of discovery, not of justification, and so need not be known to be true, or even probable. But, on the other hand, scientific hypotheses are also not *completely* random guesses: scientists strive to come up with "good guesses" that at least fit the known facts. Unfortunately, however, this analogy does not help the Designer, since the features that make for a good scientific hypothesis – one that "fits the known facts" – are not applicable to the products of Design. For example, good scientific hypotheses have high explanatory power: a hypothesis that can explain various empirical data is viewed as superior to one that leaves such data mysterious.[18] Design products, not being representations but objects for practical use, cannot be assessed in these terms.

It seems, then, that we cannot simply deny that good Designers must have justified belief in the feasibility of their solutions. Another way to respond to the problem is to show that some Designers, at least, do have such justified belief. One way to do this is to ask more specifically just what this belief must amount to. In some cases, performing a certain task with a rational expectation of success clearly requires some explicit knowledge. For example, if you don't know, at least roughly, how a combustion engine works, then you probably won't be able to fix one. But other tasks can apparently be performed, with a sound expectation of success, without any such analogous knowledge. Consider riding a bicycle, or playing the violin. Most people who can do these things cannot really explain why the things they do "work," yet they undeniably do. Philosophers capture this idea by drawing a distinction between two kinds of knowledge: *knowing that* and *knowing how* (Ryle 1946). One knows that a combustion engine works in such and such a way, but one knows how to play the violin.

Design has often been characterized as involving knowing how, rather than knowing that. This view is developed in detail in the work of Donald Schön (1983). Schön develops this idea in response to a view that he calls "Technical Rationality." According to this view, Design "consists in instrumental problem solving made rigorous by the application of scientific theory and technique" (1983, 21). Something like this view underlies the epistemological problem we have posed for Design, which insists that Designers need empirical knowledge that grounds the feasibility of their plans. Schön thought that we should reject Technical Rationality, and instead conceive of Design, not on the model of scientific knowledge, but as a form of know-how, or, as he puts it, "knowing in action" (1983, 49). Perhaps if we conceive of Design in this way, we can reject the demand for empirical knowledge that grounds the epistemological objection. We might say that, just as someone who can ride a bike cannot really explain why her actions succeed in moving the bike, but yet knows how to move the bike, the Designer cannot really explain why her Designs solve Design problems, but yet knows how to solve them.[19]

Like the creativity response discussed above, this response to the problem is attractive, because know-how does play an important role in what Designers do. For example, an architect attempts to design a transit terminal, and finds that his first efforts fail. But, after a while, he "gets the knack" for it. Perhaps he isn't really able to fully articulate the basis for why his Designs are now good ones. Nonetheless, he is able to produce them, and furthermore he can be confident that they are good Designs – ones likely to work – because he has developed this brand of "know-how."

This kind of know-how is certainly a part of Design (as well as many other activities). But an appeal to it does not resolve the epistemological problem. For the kind of know-how at issue takes shape only by virtue of a continued trial-and-error procedure carried out on the same problem. One learns how to ride a bike by getting on a bike, falling off, getting on again, falling off, and so on. Analogously, the Designer learns how to design a transit terminal by designing one, failing, designing another one, failing again and so on until he "gets it." However, when we view Design in this way, the essential elements of novelty and problem solving fall out of the picture. For the creations of our hypothetical Designer are not really new designs, but merely implementations of an established type. Design in this manner collapses into something more akin to tradition-based craft, with its emphasis on the skilful repetition of established types.

Undoubtedly some of the work that Designers do is of this nature. Nonetheless, the central part of Design practice – what makes it distinct from tradition-based craft – involves taking up truly novel problems and cases. If so, then it is not clear how the Designer can develop a kind of know-how that would justify confidence in her solutions. For experience with one type of problem does not make us capable of resolving a different kind of problem, just as making a single attempt to play ten different musical instruments does not produce the ability to play an eleventh. Here it is relevant to consider the range of different problem types tackled by many of the "great names" in Design. Raymond Loewy, for example, produced designs for corporate logos, soda bottles, automobiles, diesel trains, airplanes, refrigerators, battleships, teapots and a space station (Loewy 1988). If Loewy indeed produced these by virtue of his know-how, it remains mysterious how he, or anyone else, could acquire this capacity across such a wide and varied range of problems.

2.6 Prestructures and Principles

This difficulty – Design's focus on solving new problems, or at least solving problems in new ways – comes clearly to the fore in relation to another possible solution to the epistemological problem. In their paper "Knowledge and design," Hillier et al. (1972) confront the apparent intractability of Design problems. They observe that solving Design problems seems to require much empirical information that is typically not at the Designer's disposal. So how, they ask, is Design then possible? Their answer is that Designers proceed, and can only proceed, by employing what they call "prestructures." The prestructure "acts as a kind of plan for finding a route through problem material that would otherwise appear undifferentiated and amorphous" (9). "The notion of prestructuring," they write, "is necessary to any conceptualization of design" (7; see also Hillier and Leaman 1974).

These "prestructures" can be understood in a variety of ways. On one account, they are something like solution types that Designers can deploy when they encounter a problem. Schön, for example, discusses "design types," which he describes as "particulars that function in a general way": examples include "New England green," or "pavilion" (1988, 183). These types, Schön says, can guide the Design process: "by invoking a type, a designer can *see* how a possible design move might be matched or mismatched to a situation" (1988, 183).

This idea often surfaces in an analogy that recurs frequently in writing on the Design process: the analogy between good Designers and chess masters. The Designer is, Schön says, "like a chess master who develops a feeling for the constraints and potentials of certain configurations of pieces on the board" (1983, 104; see also Cross 2011, 146–7). We can develop the analogy by noting that chess masters deploy tactics: these are ideas that "work" in many different situations. The simplest example is the "fork": attacking two of your opponent's pieces with one of your own. Your opponent can save one piece, but loses the other, leaving you with a material advantage. What chess masters acquire is the ability to spot situations where a given tactic can be successfully employed. Although each chess position is a novel one that the master has never encountered before, the master spots features that call for certain tactics.

By analogy, we might say that the prestructures possessed by the good Designer consist in a repertoire of "design tactics," or, as Bryan Lawson (2004) calls them, "solution chunks" or "schemata," which can be abstracted from, and applied to, all sorts of particular Design situations. One of Lawson's examples is an architect's strategy of organizing an interior space around an atrium. This tactic doesn't apply only to one sort of building: it can be employed in a variety of contexts. The experienced Designer recognizes features of a unique architectural situation that call for the atrium approach, and deploys it, just as the chess master recognizes that a particular chess position calls for a tactic such as a fork, and deploys it.

There is no doubt that, through their experience with various Design problems, Designers learn these sorts of tactics, and can recognize situations where they may be deployed. But, again, it remains unclear whether this fact addresses the epistemological problem. For the question is not "Can a tactic be deployed in this situation?" but rather "Is this tactic likely to be successful in this situation?" With respect to *this* question, it is not so clear that the analogy between chess and Design holds enough water. In the case of chess, the chess master can be confident that playing a fork will lead to success because, despite the fact that they differ from each other, all chess situations are highly similar in certain fundamental ways. The same rules hold for every chess position; the ultimate aim of each player is the same for every chess position; the moves possible for any given piece are the same in each chess position. It is this similarity of all chess situations that gives the chess master confidence in deploying his repertoire of tactics.

In the case of Design, the situation is quite different. Different Design problems are not like different chess positions. The rules, aims and possibilities that hold for one situation may be entirely absent in another, even one that superficially resembles it. For instance, the atrium arrangement may be a successful approach given one set of aims, users and possibilities. But a change in these, even a slight one, may render the approach wrong-headed. It is as if, in confronting a new position, the chess master had to consider the possibility that the rules for moving a knight might be different, or that the aim of the game is no longer to capture the king, but something else (Jones 1970, 10). Recall Schön's statement that the Designer can "*see*" that a design type is the right one for a situation (note how he italicizes this critical word). But if the problem is a novel one, then how can he "see" that this is true? Of course, to the Designer it might *seem that it is true*, but this is quite different than him *seeing that it is true*.

The chess analogy therefore shows that generally deployable tactics depend upon generally applicable rules or principles. Another case that is useful to consider here is engineering, which also has its repertoire of "tactics." In this case, the tactics are clearly based on a set of physical principles or laws grounded in empirical experience. Being a good engineer is not merely a matter of knowing the relevant laws of physics, of course. But deploying the laws of physics in formulating designs is certainly necessary for being a good engineer, and the fact that he deploys these laws allows him to have a degree of confidence in his solutions. The engineer can be sure that his bridge will stand up to its load, for example, because he can use the laws of physics to make the appropriate calculations. So the question for Design is: are there any analogous general principles that apply to Design problems, principles that could underwrite a set of generally applicable Design tactics?

Attempts have of course been made to specify general principles of Design: the Designer Dieter Rams, for example, once formulated a list of ten principles of good Design. However, many of the items of his list are not so much principles that can be implemented to produce Design solutions as mere statements of Design goals: consider his principles "Good Design makes a product useful," "Good Design is aesthetic" and "Good Design is unobstrusive." These principles are not analogous to the laws of physics used by engineers in producing structures, but to principles like "Good engineering withstands use" and "Good engineering can be easily maintained."

One area where there *do* seem to be genuine Design principles, however, is the area of utility, or functionality. Donald Norman, for example, argues that a fundamental principle of Design is "make things visible" (1988, 13). Norman offers numerous examples of everyday artefacts that are difficult to use because the number of functions outstrips the number of controls, requiring the user to memorize combinations of controls, or because the controls are aligned in a way that is not visually intuitive. These failures of Design can be avoided by adding more controls, or laying the controls out in a way that is spatially intuitive for the user, drawing on scientific research in disciplines such as ergonomics. So perhaps we can say that good Designers are those who know, and deploy, these sorts of principles.

This view takes the Design problem to be a problem of functionality, or useability. As we saw earlier, however, function is only one aspect of the Design problem: the Designer has other aspects to consider as well, such as the symbolic or expressive nature of the object, as well as its aesthetic and mediating roles. Furthermore, functionality and these other aspects can easily come into conflict. For example, certain aesthetic and expressive "looks" involve a stripped-down, streamlined appearance, which conflicts directly with Norman's "make it visible" principle: the more controls that one makes visible on a device, the less stripped-down it will look. Commenting on this sort of conflict, Norman advises: "don't let the focus on cost, or durability, or aesthetics destroy the major point [of the design]: to be used" (155). But in many cases of Design, the expressive qualities, the aesthetic value or the cost effectiveness of a product can be very important – even part, one might say, of its "major point." It is not clear that Norman-style principles can give the Designer any confidence here.

Before concluding our discussion of the epistemological problem for Design, it is worth taking stock of what the problem does, and does not, mean. It does not mean that Design is impossible, nor even that good Design is impossible. Indeed, there clearly is much good Design around us (though also much that is not so good). Rather, the problem is that, when we consider the nature of Design problems, it is hard to see how anyone could be a good Designer. This produces something of a paradox: how could we have good Design but no good Designers? One explanation would be the idea, which we discussed above, that Designers merely offer random solutions – shots in the dark, as it were – with good and bad solutions being distinguished by their marketplace performance. However, this explanation is difficult to square with the fact that some people – Raymond Loewy or Henry Dreyfuss, for example – simply seem to be better at producing Design solutions. It seems implausible to attribute their success to mere blind luck.

There remain alternatives. One is returning to the traditional view that good Designers possess an intuitive "feel for the problem" that allows them to somehow obtain the right solution. Another is changing our conception of the nature of the Design problem so as to emphasize the search for functionality and downplay other aspects such as symbolism and aesthetics, where any guiding principles are harder to find. In the next chapter, we examine this second strategy, which historically has exerted a great influence on Design through the various ideas and movements that we generally refer to as "Modernism."

3

Modernism

In the previous chapter we considered the epistemological difficulties characteristic of Design problems. In this chapter we turn to an approach that promises to alleviate those difficulties. This approach emerges from an intellectual movement that has played a central role in the history of Design: Modernism. This was a movement that swept across many fields in the early years of the twentieth century, but here our focus is on its role as a philosophical position. In this regard, Modernism supported a rational conception of Design in two ways. First, it offered a reinterpretation of some of the key criteria of Design – the functional, the symbolic and the mediating – and rejected certain other interpretations of them as irrelevant. Second, it claimed to find important linkages between these criteria, linkages that might facilitate the Designer's effort to satisfy them all. To appreciate these two ways in which Modernist thought reconstrued Design problems, it is useful to first understand the origin and nature of the Modernist movement in Design.

3.1 The Origins of Modernism

The roots of Modernist thinking about Design lie outside what we might today think of as the realm of Design proper, in the nineteenth-century impulse for social reform, which was itself a reaction to the social upheaval of the industrial revolution.[1] By the early nineteenth century, industrial production had transformed the landscape and social fabric of Europe, producing large and impoverished urban working classes who performed industrial work that often was not only meaningless but dangerous. In the meantime, the bourgeois industrialists of the rising middle class made enormous profits and acquired unprecedented political power. Amidst this social change, industrial production itself produced a flood of new goods that altered the material world in which people lived. In response to these social conditions, various reform movements were established in politics, law and labor to agitate for improved working conditions and political rights and freedoms.

One of the basic insights of this reform movement was that, with the decline of craft and the rise of industrial production, a certain human element in society had been lost. The autonomy of the craftsperson, and his relation to the objects he produced as well as to the society that produced him, were being displaced. The large-scale industrial and institutional forces responsible, moreover, seemed detached not only from individuals and traditions but from each other, with each proceeding according to its own inevitable, internal "logic."[2] Social critics such as Marx saw in industrial European society a profound alienation of the individual from his fellow men, and from the very material world in which he lived.[3]

The reformist impulse to combat this situation found many outlets, but it was channeled toward Design by writers such as William Morris and John Ruskin in Britain, and Horatio Greenough in the USA. These writers drew a connection between the sorts of things that society made (and how it made them) and the quality of people's lives. Driven by their social concerns, these writers raised philosophical questions about the aim of Design, and the sorts of functionality, aesthetic value, and expression or symbolism it should pursue.

One aspect of the connection between Design and these larger social issues was the impact on those involved in mass-producing consumer goods. Some thought that the modern capitalist system of mass production was to blame for widespread social ills, and advocated a return to a more traditional and authentic craftsperson-like mode of production. In much socialist thought, traditional craft work was often contrasted, approvingly, with the alienating drudgery of the factory.

A second dimension of the connection, more spiritual than practical, involved the impact of mass production on the *consumer*. In

Britain, the Arts and Crafts movement, led by William Morris, repudiated machine production on aesthetic grounds, arguing that mass-produced goods were poorly Designed, and hopelessly inferior to the products of pre-industrial craftsmanship. Their shoddy worksmanship was disguised by the fact that they were, as a later writer put it, "submerged in cheap decoration" done in period styles intended to appeal to bourgeois ideas of good Taste.[4] Morris, who was also a leading figure in the Socialist movement, was influential in promoting the traditional craftsman model through his public lectures and the work of his firm, Morris, Marshall, Faulkner and Company, in the 1860s and 1870s (MacCarthy 1995).

Other reformers shared Morris's concerns about shoddy goods and poor working conditions in industrial Europe but not his revulsion at machines and mass production. Indeed, the development of unprecedented mechanical forms such as the steam locomotive and the iron bridge gave rise to a growing sense of the beauty of machines (see, e.g., Ewald ([1925–6] (1975)). Some saw in the modern system of machines and rationalized mass production the possibility not only for beauty but also for progressive, and indeed revolutionary, social change. The realization dawned that, within this system of mass production, the Designer's ability to create affordable and functional objects for vast markets represented an unprecedented power for social renewal. It was in this context that Modernist ideas took shape.

This account of Modernism's reformist origins emphasizes two of its key features. The first is that Modernism was, from its beginnings, a normative movement, which sought to identify not merely popular Design but *good* Design. Morris, for instance, was quite aware of the popularity of mass-produced Victorian goods; his point was that they were irremediably bad. The second feature of note here is that Modernism did not isolate Design from other activities, but rather connected it with them. It did not view itself as merely proposing a new style or mode for material goods; rather, Modernism in Design was but one facet of an entire approach to life in the "modern" era of technology and mass production (Gropius 1965, 92). The Modernist impulse was not merely to update or modernize the Design of everyday objects; more fundamentally, it sought to break down the traditional distinctions between Design and other fields of human activity, to achieve what the historian

Paul Greenhalgh (1990, 8) calls a "decompartmentalization of human experience." Walter Gropius, a central Modernist figure and founder of the Bauhaus school, which embodied many of the movement's principles, wrote that "the idea of the fundamental unity underlying all branches of design was my guiding inspiration in founding the original Bauhaus" (1965, 51). Modernist notions about Design, therefore, cannot be easily detached from broader views about politics, art and human nature – on the contrary, they were intimately bound up with them.

One important aspect of this was Modernism's contempt for the traditional, hierarchical division between the products employed in everyday life, such as furniture and tools, and so-called works of fine art. By the latter half of the nineteenth century, this distinction was well entrenched, with the fine arts, such as music, painting and sculpture, being openly celebrated for their splendid uselessness. The Aesthetic movement, also known as the "Art for Art's Sake" movement, insisted that fine art was distinct from everyday products precisely in needing to serve no utilitarian purpose, being valuable merely for "its own sake": as Oscar Wilde ([1891] 2003) memorably put it, "All art is quite useless." Modernist thinkers, however, viewed the products of fine art through the same lens of social concern that they employed in viewing the products of mass production, and from this perspective they found the fine arts to be in a rather decadent state. Gropius, for instance, attacked the view of art that "arbitrarily elevated some of its branches above the rest of the 'Fine Arts', and in doing so robbed all of their basic identity and common life" (1965, 58). The Art for Art's Sake movement sought to detach art from all practical and utilitarian concern, rejecting technical and commercial experience and insisting rather that the artist follow, and give vent to, his inner genius. This movement had been disastrous because, as Gropius caustically put it, barely one in a thousand "artists" possesses any such inner genius. As a result, this movement has only "brought about the artist's complete isolation from the community," producing a generation of "hapless drones" who, with the proper technical instruction, "could have become useful members of society" (1965, 61). Modernist thinkers therefore rejected the idea that Design should try to assimilate itself to the more prestigious fine arts. Le Corbusier, for instance, insisted that "a chair is no way a work of art; a chair has no soul; it is a machine for sitting in" ([1931] 1986, 142).

What the Modernists sought, therefore, was not to turn Design into "fine art" or tradition-based craft, but to blend the best elements of traditional craftsmanship, modern mass production and fine art into a new way of producing material goods that made sense in the social context of contemporary life. Modernist theorists pursued this aim not only in their writings, but also in their Design practice. The most famous instance of this was the operation of the Bauhaus school of Weimar Germany between 1919 and 1933. Founded by the architect Walter Gropius, the Bauhaus introduced a new approach to Design, in which students learned the techniques of both "art" and "craft," and experimented with new forms for everyday objects (Wingler 1962).

In these heady days, the Designer took on the role of social visionary, a role that had come to be associated with the fine artist during the Romantic movement a century earlier. The English poet Percy Shelley captured this view in his famous claim, "Poets are the unacknowledged legislators of the world" ([1840] 1988, 297). Unlike the artist, however, the Designer would not merely provide poetical images of a blissful future to come; he would actually bring that future into material reality. In this context, the notion of good Design, as opposed to merely popular Design, takes on a central importance. While the Designer's reformist aim is to improve the lot of the masses and society as a whole, this task is not to be carried out merely by creating popular items, for the masses themselves might well be unaware of what they need. Rather than follow contemporary taste, the Designer must lead the way by delivering items of genuine quality – good Design. In this way, Modernism puts forth a bold, humanist response to the set of problems posed by the industrial revolution. The mechanical, institutional processes of industrial mass production might continue to grind away, but they would now have a soul: a *human being* guiding it all, and us, to a better future.

3.2   Reinterpretations and Linkages

Our description of Modernism in Design has omitted much detail and glossed over many subtleties, but gives a sense of its origins and ambitions. How did Modernists attempt to realize their lofty goals? As we have discussed in chapter 2, solving Design problems

– producing good Designs – is fraught with a basic epistemological difficulty. One response to this problem – admittedly not very attractive – is to return to the old idea that good Designers possess a special intuition. Modernist thinking, however, addresses the problem in a different way, by inviting us to reconceive the very nature of Design problems.

Before we examine this approach, however, a caveat is in order. Although I will draw on historical sources, what I aim to give here is not an account that was held by all Modernist thinkers, or even by any particular one. Rather, the aim here is to provide a "rational reconstruction" of the central set of ideas that characterize the movement as a whole.[5] That is, we will not be primarily interested in working out the actual views of any particular Modernist figure or school, but rather in trying to extract from their statements a cogent theoretical position on Design. Our "reconstruction" of Modernism will thus doubtless appear to be a gross over-simplification of the actual views and practice of any particular historical figure. This level of abstraction is necessary, however, if we are to examine Modernist ideas philosophically, as a general approach to Design.

The first, and boldest, way in which Modernism reconceives of the nature of Design problems is by radically reinterpreting the symbolic or the expressive as a criterion for good Design. Perhaps the classic and most powerful example of this in Modernist writing is the essay "Ornament and crime" (1908) by the Austrian architect Adolf Loos.[6] Loos's essay is an attack on contemporary taste in consumer goods, which he decries as beset by "the ornament disease." Decoration or adornment – expressive features that bear no relation to an item's utilitarian purpose – are to be rejected. Good Design, Loos's account suggests, creates objects that are simply functional and useful, devoid of such adornment. Loos admits that many of his contemporaries enjoy Design that is highly ornamental – the Vienna in which Loos lived and wrote was dominated by it. Its two main Design trends were Historicism, which employed traditional and highly ornamental styles from specific historical periods, and the reactionary Art Nouveau style of the Viennese Secession, both of which indulged in rather wild forms of ornamentation (Schorske 1980). However, Loos argues that such Design, though popular, is nonetheless poor Design. To put it another way, he might say that people with a taste for highly ornamental or decorated items have bad Taste in Design.

Loos's essay is highly polemical and (though this is sometimes overlooked) satirical, castigating ornament not only as a disease and a crime (as in his title), but also as an epidemic and a form of slavery. At times, he appears to simply state his view, confident that the reader will recognize its truth immediately: "All modern people will [understand me]," he declares ([1908] 1970, 60). But Loos also offers some reasons in support of his claim that good Design eschews ornament. The first of these is that for contemporary or, as Loos puts it, "modern" man, ornamentation has been superseded by superior forms of cultural expression. Loos bases this claim on two ideas.[7]

The first idea is that ornamentation, in all its manifestations, emerges from a single impulse belonging to human nature, the erotic impulse. The notion that artistic activity has a deep root in sexual instinct was a current one in Loos's *fin-de-siècle* Vienna, where Freud was formulating theories of human psychology rooted in the repression of the sexual instinct. The style of Art Nouveau, with its sensuous curves, also had an apparent erotic element, most famously exemplified in the work of Secession artists such as Klimt and Schiele. Loos extends the notion of the erotic impulse, connecting it to the ornamentation of everyday goods, such as women's fashions: "Woman covered herself," Loos writes, "and thereby made herself a mystery to man in order to fill his heart with a longing to solve the mystery" ([1898c] 2011, 63). The restless alteration in the ornamentation of women's clothing, for Loos, reflects this constant attempt to generate an erotic attractiveness.

Loos's second idea is that the means available for expressing the erotic impulse can be better or worse in relation to a given culture. Thus Loos holds that the ornamentation of everyday goods is a natural and proper outlet for expressing the erotic impulse in certain cultures (his examples include traditional Maori culture and the peasant culture of his own rural Austria). Ornamenting everyday things, in these cultures, is a valid way of giving them a meaning and allure that renders them more appealing. In the metropolitan culture of his Vienna, however, Loos thought that it was an inferior outlet for expressing the same impulse. The impulses that once found expression in the ornamentation of everyday things now had better outlets – as he put it, humanity (i.e., contemporary European culture) has "outgrown ornament" ([1908] 1970, 20).[8]

Loos's account immediately suggests a reinterpretation of the criterion of expression or symbolism for Design. Traditionally, the

Designer worried not merely about how to Design an object that would function, but how to create an object that would "say" whatever it needed to "say." Thus, on top of the functional dimension of the Design product the Designer typically superimposed a symbolic or expressive layer of ornament that would convey the required message, and make it more alluring and desirable. This is the layer of ornament against which Morris had reacted so viscerally in Victorian design. Loos's idea in "Ornament and crime" is that we should simply eliminate this additional layer of concern for the Designer.[9]

Although this point does not come out in "Ornament and crime," it is important to note that this position – the rejection of ornament – does not thereby eliminate the expressive or symbolic dimension of Design products: Design products could still "say" something, or express an idea or content, via their functional elements. This notion – that Design products can be expressive or symbolic without ornamentation – is key to the Modernist view of design: without it, Modernism could produce goods that were useful but without any significance or meaning. Such a radical view would be very unintuitive.[10] Modernists, however, saw the elimination of ornament not as an impoverishment of the symbolic or expressive aspect of Design, but as an enrichment of it.

How exactly were unornamented design products expressive? The key idea here is that they were to be, as Walter Gropius put it, the "concrete expression of the life of our epoch" (1965, 44; see also 89). Freed from ornament, Design products would express the *Zeitgeist*, or the true "spirit of the age." Here Modernists looked to the way that the great architecture of past cultures – Egypt, Greece, Rome – seemed to effortlessly express the particular way of life characteristic of each of these civilizations. The thought was that, in our time, the use of ornamental styles from the past could not express the spirit of *our* culture, but only obscure it. Only by eschewing such frippery and creating functional designs could we express our age in the way that the Greek temple or the Roman forum expressed theirs.[11]

The architectural historian Nikolaus Pevsner, in his famous account of the origins of the Modernist movement, elaborated on the expressiveness of its products:

It is the creative energy of this world in which we live and work and which we want to master, a world of science and technology, of speed

and danger, of hard struggles and no personal security, that is glori-
fied in [Modernist works such as] Gropius's architecture, and as long
as this is the world and these are its ambitions and problems, the
style of Gropius . . . will be valid. ([1936] 2011, 163)

Only in Modernist architecture, Pevsner said, does "today's reality"
find its "complete expression." This expression emerges naturally,
inevitably, when contemporary materials and methods are employed
to produce objects that are functional for contemporary life. In this
sense expressiveness is produced almost as a by-product of satisfying
the functional requirements of Design problems.

"Ornament and crime" also exemplifies a second way in which
Modernist thinking tended to simplify Design problems: by identifying conceptual linkages between the criteria of functionality and
beauty, or aesthetic value. Given that he rejects ornamentation or
decoration outright, Loos might be thought to be simply dismissing
aesthetic value as irrelevant to Design as well. But, like the claim
that good Design is meaningless, the notion that good Design
should have no beauty is very unintuitive. Accordingly, Loos is
careful to insist that his rejection of ornament is not a "mortifica-
tion": that is, not merely a Puritanical or ascetic renunciation of
pleasure or aesthetics. Rather, he claims that the "modern man"
really prefers simple, undecorated forms *on aesthetic grounds*: "I am
not denying myself!" he declares. Loos thus sees himself not as
urging a rejection of aesthetics, or as describing yet another style,
but as presenting a philosophical discovery about the nature of true
aesthetic value in consumer goods.

Here Modernism taps into a long-standing tradition that views a
thing's functionality, or its fitness for its purpose, as giving rise to
beauty or aesthetic appeal. Loos maintains that "the highest degree
of functionality in harmony with all the other parts [of an object] is
what we call pure beauty" ([1898a] 1982, 29).[12] This tradition
extends back as far as the ancient Greeks: Socrates, for example, was
supposed to have claimed, "Whatever is useful we call beautiful."[13]
Although this view experienced a decline in the philosophical
thought of the late eighteenth and early nineteenth century, it was
simultaneously being rejuvenated, in a wider context, by the development of spectacular machines such as the steam engine, which
Umberto Eco cites as the "definite advent of aesthetic enthusiasm
for the machine" (2005, 293).[14] Writing in the 1920s, the German

writer Kurt Ewald summed up the new perspective this way: "Modern machines are built on purely functional lines, with the purpose of achieving a given performance with the most economical – which means the most perfect – means. The more consciously and methodically this aim is pursued, the more practically and functionally the construction of the machine will be conceived and the more satisfying will be its aesthetic effect" ([1925–6] 1975, 145).[15] This view implies that there is a happy harmony between the criteria of functionality and aesthetic value in Design. Once again, a criterion of good Design (in this case, aesthetic value) is satisfied as a by-product of satisfying the criterion of functionality.

Although it is less developed, we can also discern the outlines of a similar move in "Ornament and crime," with respect to what we have called the mediating criterion for Design. In a general sense, mediation refers to Design's impact upon our patterns of life, and larger social and political concerns that pertain to them. Loos touches on this area in suggesting that the ornamentation of everyday objects is objectionable because of its waste of labor, time and expense, being, as he puts it, "a crime against the national economy" ([1908] 1970, 21). "Ornament," he writes, "is wasted labor power and hence wasted health" (22). In a passage with a remarkably contemporary ring, Loos bemoans the waste caused by fashion's constant adoption of ever new, but ultimately meaningless, ornamental styles, a cycle that causes furniture to be replaced every few years in accord with shifting tastes. Here again the idea emerges that there is a sort of fortunate alignment or linkage between the aim of functionality and the aims of mediating human life: merely by producing goods that are functional and useful, the designer will improve the fabric of human life.

Overall, our account of Modernism's "reconceptualization" of Design problems is nicely summed up in the famous slogan "Form follows Function." The central idea is that if the Designer merely constructs the object to perform its function, then expression, aesthetic value and mediation become, as it were, "spin-off" values that follow effortlessly.[16] When coupled with the idea – explored in chapter 2 – that the Designer can have access to reliable general principles when it comes to function, the allure of the Modernist vision becomes plain. By focusing on producing functional goods, Designers can rationally tackle the problems that confront them, creating a material world that is not only useful but meaningful, socially progressive and beautiful.

3.3   The Failure of Modernism?

As a historical movement, Modernism has had a highly disputed legacy, to put it mildly. Modernist notions of good Design had an indisputable effect upon the look and character of architecture and consumer goods in the early twentieth century as the simpler, unadorned forms favored by Modernists came into vogue.[17] In architecture, Modernism resulted in the so-called "International Style," which still dominates the skyline of many cities today. But the utopian visions of Modernist theory were only one force driving the development of Design. An equally – if not more – potent force was Design's commercial dimension. As theorists such as Loos and Gropius were writing their manifestos, corporations were busy hiring artists to run Design departments and sell unfamiliar products to a skeptical public. Although "modern" forms had attained broad cultural appeal, the market continued to demand more traditional ornamental styles as well.

For example, as Thomas Hine documents in his book *Populuxe* (1986), a prosperous postwar America embraced an exuberantly ornamental material culture, despite the protests of outraged Modernists. One example is the use of ornamentation for the automobile in the 1950s: cars were given ostentatious fins as a way of evoking the speed, technological prestige and romance of the jet aircraft. Under this commercial pressure, Modernism's cherished ideals of "good Design" could seem like an unreal abstraction: "Good Design," went the quip, "is an upward sales curve."

In addition to this ongoing pushback from bourgeois tastes in the marketplace, Modernism faced problems from within, as high-profile efforts in architecture by leading Modernist figures, such as Le Corbusier, came under criticism. The most famous of these failures was the Pruitt–Igoe housing complex, built in St. Louis in the early 1950s. The project applied Modernist ideas on a massive scale, consisting of thirty-three eleven-story towers. Although the project was designed to provide improved living conditions for people who had lived in "slum areas," the towers quickly became dilapidated and crime-ridden. Residents fled, and the authorities decided that the project was better off demolished than rehabilitated; the first tower was destroyed in 1972, an event that Charles Jencks later famously hailed as "the day that Modernist architecture died" (1991, 23).[18] In the wake of such failures, critics of Modernism in architecture, such as Robert Venturi, now lamented, rather than celebrated, the "total control" of the Designer (Venturi et al. 1977, 149). In *From Bauhaus to Our House* (1981), the American writer Tom Wolfe lampooned the by-now passé pretensions of Modernism.

Speaking very generally, we can reconstruct, from these trends, a reactionary theoretical position about Design. Like Modernism itself, this position appeared in innumerable variations, but the idea at its core is a rejection of the notion of good Design as opposed to popular Design. As we have seen, this distinction is at the heart of Modernism: Modernists articulate a conception of what Design *ought* to do, and, at least roughly, provide some ways in which the requisite kind of products can be realized. The theoretical position under discussion now, in contrast, eschews a normative conception of Design. It is tempting to call this position "post-Modernism"; but this term has been used so variously that so employing it would, perhaps, only court confusion. More importantly, this term is a loaded one, implying that Modernism has, in some sense, "ended," which begs the entire question as to whether Modernist ideas still have any validity. So let us instead call this the "Pluralist conception" of Design.

A very forceful account of this view is Virginia Postrel's book *The Substance of Style* (2003). Although not explicitly philosophical, Postrel's book is a sustained and well-informed attempt to think through the current state of Design and the fate of the Modernist legacy. Postrel claims that ours is an age of "aesthetic pluralism" that "overthrows modernist ideology" (13). In opposition to Loos's idea that humanity has outgrown the need to ornament everyday artefacts, Postrel insists that the adornment of consumer goods is a natural and irresistible aesthetic impulse. And the aesthetic impulse, she insists, is subjective: the proper locution today is "'I like that' rather than 'This is good design'" (10). Modernism, despite its pretensions to have discovered the true nature of aesthetic value, was really only another style. We should treat Designed items, she urges, as we treat food, where "the diner, not the cook, is the ultimate arbiter of what works" (7). In Postrel's view, Design today enjoys a Golden Age, not because it produces "good Designs," but because of its capacity to offer an enormous array of custom options, sure to please each and every taste.

A similar view is reached, from a slightly different direction, by the Design writer Gert Selle (1984) in his defense of pedestrian everyday objects that, falling short of the Design elite's conceptions of "good Design," are denigrated as "tacky" or ugly. These are precisely the sort of wildly ornamental goods against which Morris and Gropius reacted. The best that Modernism can say about such objects is that they are enjoyable in a perverse way, when viewed as "kitsch" – that is, when enjoyed precisely for how comically awful and vulgar they are. Against this view, Selle writes that "there simply is no absolute 'good taste.' It exists only in relation to a basis of social points of departure, that is, everyone who lives according to his taste has a 'good taste,' which, of course, can be distinguished from another 'good taste'" (1984, 49). Like Postrel, Selle emphasizes the failure of Modernism to win universal acceptance. Modernist attempts to promote so-called "good Design" have, he says, "run into a void," and been "brilliantly withstood."

Views such as Postrel's and Selle's seem compelling.[19] After all, as mentioned above, it is true that Modernist approaches to Design did not win universal acceptance. It is also true that the "kitschy" everyday objects that Postrel and Selle celebrate, which seem to fall short of Modernist ideals, can be attractive and aesthetically pleasing. However, the question is whether these facts undermine Modernism, or the very notion of good Design, as these authors would conclude. In this regard, the arguments given by Postrel and Selle have an odd ring to them.

This comes out nicely in Selle's remark that the idea that all tastes are equally valid "has prevailed with the normative power of the factual" (1984, 52). The idea seems to be that the fact that people favor different kinds of Design products, and do not agree on what constitutes good Design, proves, or at least supports, the conclusion that there is no such thing as good Design. But this "normative power of the factual" would be a strange power indeed, for how can the *descriptive* fact that people reject a *normative* statement show it to be false? As an analogy, we might consider the claim that "stealing is wrong." The fact that a large group of people, or even an entire culture, rejected that claim would not, in itself, seem to have any bearing on whether or not that statement is true. Rather, it would seem that, to determine whether the statement is true or false, we must consider the reasons for and against it. To do otherwise is to commit what philosophers call the "naturalistic fallacy": making the mistaken inference from what *is* the case to what *ought to be* the case. Another way to put this point is to say that this "rejection of Modernism" offered by Postrel and Selle is not really a rejection of Modernism at all, but simply a changing of the subject, from good Design to popular Design.

In this regard, it is worth noting that Postrel's and Selle's rejections of Modernism largely cast the discussion in terms of "taste," or preferences as to what is beautiful or aesthetically appealing. This is typical of wholesale rejections of Modernism: another critic describes Modernism as "a set of arbitrary, systematized aesthetic choices" (Brolin 1976, 13). This shift of focus to aesthetics makes the rejection of Modernism more plausible, since it is received wisdom that aesthetic preferences differ and it is a common dictum that there is "no accounting for Tastes." Be this as it may (as we will see in chapter 6, it may not be), while beauty or aesthetic value is *one* criterion for Design, it is far from the only one, and Modernists did not see their conception of good Design as a solely aesthetic choice. Rather, they viewed their conception of good Design as emerging from consideration of the whole of contemporary life, and in particular the place of ornament in it. As such, a rejection of the Modernist vision ought to take issue with this consideration as a whole, not merely with one aspect of it.

The point made above, that Modernism is a normative view rather than a descriptive one, is enough to show that the rejection of Modernism on offer fails. However, something further can be said. So far, we have been granting critics of Modernism such as Postrel and Selle a key premise, which is that Modernism's notion of good Design *has* been rejected by the masses: "overthrown" and "brilliantly withstood," as Selle puts it. A common theme in discussions of Modernism is that it was conceived as a reactionary strike against the vulgar bourgeois, or upper middle classes, by "artistic and intellectual elites" (Brolin 1976, 20). The idea is that, once mass-produced items became widely available to the middle classes, Modernism was concocted to restrain their natural taste for ornament, as a way of putting people with more money than culture in their place. The masses did not really want Modernist designs – they secretly loathed them – but, insecure about their social position, they felt obligated to follow the dictates of elites. And so, as Tom Wolfe put it, when Modernist Designs were suggested, they "took it like a man" (1981, 143).[20] But is it true that "the people" really wanted ornamental design, and rejected Modernist Design?

Certainly there is a plurality of preferences in Design, as in most things. But how thorough is this disagreement? Critics of Modernism emphasize the failures of Modernism, but tend to ignore the successes. Many Modernist creations have become undisputed "Design classics" (Parsons 2013, 621). Consider Harry Beck's brilliantly lucid map of the London Underground system, briefly scrapped in the 1950s only to be reinstated due to *popular* demand. Today it is an icon of Modern graphic design and the model for most underground maps around the world (Forty [1986] 2005). Or, consider the popularity of the products produced by Apple, which manifest Modernist principles.[21] Of course it is easy to find examples of Modernist designs that failed to win praise (it is noteworthy that discussions of the failure of Modernism tend to focus on architecture). And even for Modernist successes like the Beck map, there are dissenters. But rejecting Modernism, as an approach to Design, on these grounds would be like rejecting the scientific method because some scientific theories fail or because no theory is ever accepted by everyone.

Perhaps more importantly, it is not only products of Modernist Design that have had lasting appeal and influence, but also its principles. Consider again Dieter Rams's ten "Principles of good Design," mentioned in chapter 2. We pointed out there that these principles are perhaps better described as descriptions of Design aims or goals, rather than as methodological principles. It is easy to see the influence of Modernist thinking in what Rams has to say about these aims. For example, about utility, he says that "Products fulfilling a purpose are like tools. They are neither decorative objects nor works of art. Their design should therefore be both neutral and restrained" (Lovell 2011; see also Rawsthorn 2008).

Of course, we could also find Designers who would reject such Modernist-inspired ideas. However, the fact that some influential Designers continue to hold to them suggests that they at least deserve to be considered seriously on their merits rather than disregarded because they are not universally accepted. If universal acceptance were the criterion for acknowledging a principle as true or valid, then we would recognize no principles at all. A better approach is to scrutinize the arguments offered in support of the Modernist approach to Design, and it is to this task that we now must turn.

4

Expression

In the previous chapter, we sketched a seductive and bold reinterpretation of Design problems suggested by Modernist thinking. In this chapter, we begin a critical examination of this approach, starting with one of the most characteristic moves in Modernist thought: simplifying the expressive, or symbolic, nature of the Design problem by rejecting ornamentation. This is a move inspired by Loos's famous essay "Ornament and crime."

Modernism's eschewal of ornamentation has been subject to a great deal of criticism. This criticism has both motivated, and been motivated by, investigation of the symbolic and expressive dimensions of Design products during the last century. Theorists from a variety of disciplines have tried to explain the meaning of consumer goods in contemporary life, both for its own sake and in relation to larger questions about politics, economics, human nature and society. A good place to begin our appraisal of the Modernist approach to meaning in Design, then, is by examining what these studies have to tell us about the meaning of everyday products of Design.

4.1   The Meanings of Design

In rejecting ornament, the Modernist view, as we've seen, does not banish expression or symbolization from Design, for it allows that Design objects can be expressive, as long as the expression is managed through the functional aspect of the Design. It does, however, narrowly restrict the expressive *content* of design to the *Zeitgeist*, or "spirit of the age" in which it is produced. The idea that this restriction is too narrow is reinforced by a wide range of theories in twentieth-century social science that have tried to clarify the expressive nature, or the meaning, of Design goods.[1]

Perhaps the most influential approach in this field comes from the American sociologist Thorstein Veblen, who analyzed social interests in consumer goods in his book *The Theory of the Leisure Class* ([1899] 1994). Veblen believed that humans have an inherent desire to display their status, to make it known to others that they occupy a certain rank in the social hierarchy. In modern societies, Veblen thought, they do this by displaying wealth through the purchase of consumer goods, often ones that are quite useless when viewed from a utilitarian or an aesthetic perspective. Precisely because the goods in question are useless, this "conspicuous consumption," as Veblen called it, signals that the purchaser has financial wealth to spare and hence is of a higher social rank. Veblen's analysis suggests that we value consumer goods not only for their aesthetic value, utility or social value, but as social signals, or indicators of status.

An understanding of consumer goods as allowing individuals and groups to make class distinctions is also a theme in the work of the French sociologist Pierre Bourdieu. "Social subjects," Bourdieu wrote, are "classified by their classifications," and "distinguish themselves by the distinctions they make, between the beautiful and the ugly, the distinguished and the vulgar, in which their position in the objective classifications is expressed or betrayed" (1984, 6). Bourdieu held that one's preferences in material goods and in art are read as indicators of a person's "cultural capital": his or her understanding and awareness of the essential elements of culture. It is not merely one's ability to *pay* for things that marks one's status; for Bourdieu, the ability to appreciate and interpret certain sorts of "stylish" consumer goods itself acts as a way of establishing social status. As he puts it, "Taste classifies, and it classifies the classifier" (6).

These accounts offer an analysis of our attraction to consumer goods in terms of social relations. Another such account that is somewhat broader in scope can be found in the work of the anthropologists Mary Douglas and Baron Isherwood. In their book *The World of Goods* (1979), they see the significance of consumer goods in terms of social forces that extend beyond the individualistic desire to assert one's status. Douglas and Isherwood draw a connection between consumer goods and social rituals. In anthropology, social rituals – cult or religious ceremonies, for example – are understood as ways of making the categories and values of a culture visible and manifest. Anthropologists typically understand the material goods of other cultures in connection with these rituals, as ways in which these cultures "make and maintain social relationships" (39). "Goods," Douglas and Isherwood write, "are ritual adjuncts, [and] consumption is a ritual process whose primary function is to make sense of the inchoate flux of events." They offer the example of the Nuer culture of Sudan, which structures its social relations in terms of the ownership and exchange of cattle. Cattle are key markers of social status, but their significance extends far beyond this as virtually all aspects of Nuer life involve cattle in some way.

Douglas and Isherwood ask why this view of material objects, which is "practically axiomatic" in anthropological accounts of other cultures, is not applied to our own material possessions. They seek to remedy this inconsistency by applying the anthropological view to contemporary Western consumption. On this view, a possession like a house is not merely a functional device – "a machine for living," as Le Corbusier famously put it: it does not merely house the owner's material goods and shelter him from the elements. Neither is it merely a way of showing status, or inciting envy or respect in his neighbors. It also expresses in a visible way the person's values: a heritage home announces one's commitment to the past; a house with a pool announces one's love of leisure and the outdoors; a house with a large open kitchen makes tangible one's desire for informal socializing. The house also inserts the owner into a set of social relations, placing him within one community, excluding him from others. And finally, the house makes possible various kinds of social interactions, while excluding others: a house with a door on the sidewalk allows interaction with the street and one's neighbors, while a house set back from the street behind an expansive lawn does the opposite. In a broader way, the size and layout of one's house will determine what sort of gatherings one hosts, and consequently what kind of social interactions one can engage in. The choice involved in buying a house, then, goes far beyond considerations of function or status; it is a choice that reflects the kinds of values that help shape our lives. Buying a house is, in other words, a "ritual process" by which we give meaning and structure to the world, in the same way that religious ceremonies in other cultures studied by anthropologists serve to give meaning and structure to their ways of life.

The idea that we seek out consumer goods that will in some sense define what we believe in is picked up on by other thinkers who stress the relation of consumer goods to our own self-conception, or sense of who we are. As Herbert Marcuse (1964, 9) put it, "the people recognize themselves in their commodities; they find their soul in their automobile, hi-fi set, split-level home, kitchen equipment." Erving Goffman, in *The Presentation of the Self in Everyday Life* (1959), his classic study of the process of projecting an impression of oneself, acknowledges the role played by material possessions and surroundings in this process (22). Some theorists relate the expression of individual identity back to the sort of class distinctions characterized by theorists such as Veblen and Bourdieu. As one writer puts it, "the desire is not to be unique in the sense of total self-reliance or even social disconnection, but to achieve social status, acceptance, and a sense of belonging through the projection of individuality" (Jens 2009, 331).

Others have pointed to different psychological forces at work in consumerism. In his book *Mythologies* ([1957] 1972), the French theorist Roland Barthes explored the hidden springs of popular attraction to everyday objects and events. Of a mid-1950s automobile, the Citroen D.S., Barthes wrote that it seems to the viewer to have "fallen from the sky": lacking traces of the "typically human operation of assembling," its pieces seem to "hold together by sole virtue of their wondrous shape." This magical object appears to us as a "messenger of a world above nature" (88), a world with no purpose or meaning apart from the satisfaction of our desire for comfort. Barthes suggests that this object – the embodiment of a perfect ahistorical world dedicated to our pleasure – represents "the very essence of petit-bourgeois advancement" (90). The dream of the aspiring middle class is to assert its power over nature and society, to bend these to its will and from them reap comfort, security and prosperity. The Citroen, he suggests, beguiles the consumer because it *is* this dream, wrought in tangible form and therefore "possessable."

This basic theme – that we are attracted to Designs because they touch on or express deeply held dreams and motives – has been developed in many variations. Some writers emphasize how Design objects can speak not to our aspirations, but rather to our fears. As an example, consider Daniel Harris's essay on "quaint" décor items. The quaint encompasses things such as furniture deliberately constructed so as to appear older and thus authentically rustic; such furniture is sometimes intentionally damaged, or "distressed," to achieve this look. Our love of the quaint, Harris argues, "express[es] the discontent of a culture trapped in an eternal present, one in which everything is brand-new, squeaky clean, packaged in Styrofoam peanuts and shrink-wrapped" (2001, 35). Where Barthes considers the allure of the perfect, unearthly object, Harris focuses on its distressing or disturbing aspects. Together the two examples nicely show how complex our attractions to Design objects can be if they are a product of subconscious beliefs and emotions.

Another account of our attraction to consumer goods, that of the sociologist Colin Campbell (1989), covers similar ground but puts the concept of pleasure in the foreground. For Campbell, our central relation to consumer goods – the one that does most to explain the nature of contemporary consumer behavior – is one of pleasurable fantasy. As he puts it, "individuals do not so much seek satisfaction from products, as pleasure from the self-illusory experiences which they construct from their associated meanings" (89). We employ new Design products as opportunities for day-dreaming about new experiences and possibilities: this day-dreaming generates a longing for the object in question, but is also pleasurable in its own right, affording us a kind of control that is typically absent in the enjoyment of "real" pleasures. On Campbell's view, the distinctively imaginative enjoyment of new consumer goods explains a key feature of modern consumer desire: its apparently inexhaustible nature. For as soon as we obtain the desired item, it is no longer the perfect, gilded object of our fantasy, but merely what it really is. Hence the actual acquisition of design goods is "a necessarily disillusioning experience" and as soon as it is complete we move on to fantasize about another, as yet unattained, object of desire (86).

Taken together, this work provides a complex picture of the symbolic or expressive dimension of consumer goods.[2] While one may not accept all of the theories offered, at the very least this account lends support to the charge that the Modernist view provides us with, at best, a quite impoverished conception of this dimension.

4.2 Expression and Eros

The complex picture of Design meaning that emerges from these studies of consumerism is illuminating and important. In itself, however, it does not undercut the fundamental Modernist claim that good Design expresses only the *Zeitgeist*, since that claim is a normative one, rather than a descriptive one. That is, the claim is that, even if people *do* value goods for expressing other things, there are good reasons why they *ought* not to do so.[3] To see this, we need only recall that Loos was well aware of the popularity of extravagant ornamentation and status expression in the material culture of his society; indeed, he somewhat revels in the iconoclastic nature of his own views. To evaluate his case against expression in Design, we need to consider the arguments that might be used to support it.

As we've seen, Loos himself suggests one such argument: he rejects the expression of the "erotic impulse" in ornamentation because this impulse now has more effective outlets. It seems difficult, at first glance, even to take Loos's argument seriously in light of the contemporary understanding of the meaning of consumer goods sketched in the previous section. We may argue about some details of the broad picture emerging there, but it is hard to look at it as a whole and maintain that no more is going on in our desire for consumer goods than some sort of quasi-sexual impulse.

Closer scrutiny of Loos's notion of the "erotic impulse," however, is helpful here. To our ears, the English word "erotic" has inherently carnal overtones, calling to mind graphic representations of sex, as in "erotic literature," or "erotica." Loos uses the word *eros*, however, in its original Greek sense of a longing for something considered excellent or valuable (or as the Greeks would say, beautiful). Thus, Loos's "erotic impulse" is not merely the impulse of sexual desire, but the more fundamental desire to make oneself stand out, to be noticed and therefore attractive to others.[4] This comes out in his discussion of ornament in the context of women's fashion, which, as mentioned earlier, he sees as a device by which women compete with one another in an attempt to be noticed by men. Loos's view, properly stated, then, is that the adoption of ornament is, at bottom, an attempt at *displaying one's valuable nature*, allowing one to be noticed by, and to appeal to, others.

As we have seen, however, contemporary accounts of the meaning of consumer goods suggest that Design serves to express a great many different things. Can all ornamentation be said to be rooted in this urge to display one's valuable nature? Consider the Veblenesque idea that we are attracted to Design products that allow us to express social status, for instance. The desire to advertise status is the desire to stand apart from the crowd, to be noticed as a distinct individual worthy of admiration and regard. The idea of using ornamentation to allow the expression of personal identity fits Loos's account even more clearly: I desire goods that will not only function well for their intended purpose, but show people the interesting and distinctive person that I really am. I want my furniture to announce that I am a refined person, for example, or someone who values the heritage of the past.

What about the anthropological conception of consumer goods as "ritual adjuncts" that express or make tangible cultural values? Here again it seems plausible to see the desire to display a valuable nature as key. I value the heritage of the past, or a certain kind of informal social community, and choose to buy a certain house because it has features that will show this forth. This is not necessarily an attempt to show status, in the Veblenesque sense, but it is an attempt at displaying an important aspect of oneself: one's most important beliefs and values. It is an attempt, again, to display one's valuable nature.

We can consider also our examples of the car that expresses the bourgeois ideal toward which we aspire, and quaint objects that express comforting or reassuring ideas. Here too one might say that our attraction to these objects is based on their display of something attractive or valuable: a sense of the world as we would like it to be, tamed by reason and science in the case of the car, or still full of wholesome and dedicated craftspeople, in the case of the quaint. In the case of Campbell's theory of consumerism, a similar connection can also be made, in a more general way: we are drawn to objects that allow us to dream of a world where all our desires are fulfilled. Consumerism produces goods and services that, by their expressive qualities, feed such fantasies, offering a glimpse of the world as we long for it to be.

There are no doubt important differences amongst these various cases. In some of them, it is the valuable nature of a person that is primarily displayed, whereas in others it is the valuable nature of something broader in scope: a community or a culture, perhaps. But in all of them, the basic impulse driving the expressive dimension of Design is the same: the desire to render things attractive through "showing forth" their valuable nature. This is the sense in which, for Loos, ornament in general has its roots in the erotic impulse.

4.3   The Better Realization Argument

So far, we've been examining the first part of Loos's rejection of expressive ornament: the idea that the expressive dimension of Design is a manifestation of the erotic impulse. The second part of his view is that it is also a *sub-optimal* manifestation of it: there are more effective ("more refined, more subtle," as he puts it) ways of displaying one's valuable nature.

What could these other outlets be? If we consider first cases where Design's expressive dimension aims at displaying the valuable nature of an individual, then one answer is that person's actions, both physical and intellectual.[5] Two reasons can be given for this. First, there is a more intimate relation between a person's nature and his or her actions than there is between a person's nature and his or her possessions, insofar as our actions do not have the same "distance" from us that our possessions do. My actions have a tendency to "give away" or reveal my nature in a way that my consciously chosen possessions do not. Second, our actions tend to reinforce our tendencies and characteristics in a way that possessions do not: being athletic – swimming, running and so on – will tend to reinforce this characteristic in a way that merely possessing symbols of athleticism (athletic clothing or gear, for example) does not. Thus, again, we expect there to be a more intimate connection between a person's actions and his or her character.

Given this line of thought, then, perhaps we can reformulate Loos's argument this way:

1. Design is made expressive as a way of displaying our valuable nature.
2. The display of our valuable nature is better done by things other than expressive Design objects (namely, actions).
3. So, expression is not a good-making feature of Design.[6]

Let us call this the "Better Realization Argument" against ornament in Design. The key idea in the argument, manifested in its second premise, is that the aim of displaying our valuable nature is better realized by our actions than by the expressive ornament of Design objects.

Is this true? One might argue that it is not, on the grounds that, generally speaking, objects can communicate ideas more widely than actions can. I can, perhaps, communicate my valuable nature through my actions to people who know me, but through possessions I could communicate these same ideas to countless strangers (through, say, the car I choose to drive). However, the additional quantity of expression made possible by the use of expressive objects is not helpful if this expression is of low quality, and that is precisely the upshot of the two points offered above. Although objects are an easier means for showing ideas about oneself to others, they make reading those ideas more difficult: we can trust the character-revelation of action to a greater degree than that of possessions. So, insofar as we are concerned to communicate our valuable nature to others, we would, if we are rational, choose to do this through action.

Given the truth of the premises, the fundamental question about the argument is whether those premisses actually support its conclusion. That is, assuming that expressive Design objects are an inferior means of displaying one's valuable nature, would that give us reason to reject such expressiveness as a criterion of good Design? Another way to put this question is to ask whether the Better Realization argument is a valid one, such that, given the truth of the premises, the conclusion must be true.

As we stated it above, the argument is surely not valid. For one might concede the truth of the first two premises and yet deny the conclusion, in the following way. One might agree that expressive Design aims at displaying our valuable nature, and admit that it does this less well than action does, but still insist that expressiveness is nevertheless a good-making feature of Design. After all, one might point out that actions themselves, even if better than possessions, are hardly infallible as a means of displaying one's valuable nature: people can act in "phony" ways. Why then should the inefficiency of expressive Design goods rule out their use, when action's inefficiencies do not rule it out?

To address this issue, an additional premise will be required in order to render the argument valid, as follows:

1. Design is made expressive as a way of displaying our valuable nature.
2. If Xs have P in order to perform F, but F is done better by something else, then P is not a good-making feature of Xs.
3. The display of our valuable nature is better done by things other than expressive Design objects (namely, actions).
4. So, expression is not a good-making feature of Design.

This version of the argument is valid, meaning that its internal logic is correct: if the premises are true, then the conclusion must also be true. However, are those premises true? In particular, is the premise that we had to add – the second premise – true?

One might argue that it is false: that is, the fact that something we can do with X can be done better with something else doesn't give us reason to think that doing this thing is not a good-making feature of Xs. For example, one might suggest that, at least in many urban environments today (sprawling North American cities, for example), personal transportation is better achieved by the use of the car than by the use of a bicycle: one is safer and arrives at one's destination more rapidly by car; one can transport more items in a car; one can travel in more types of weather in a car, and so on. Of course, one can get around these urban environments on a bicycle, but one gets around more efficiently and effectively with a car. But just from this fact, it doesn't seem to follow that bicycle features that facilitate personal transportation in an urban environment – baskets for carrying parcels, splashguards and so on – are not good-making features of bicycles: we might still praise bicycles for having these features. To put it another way, the fact that the car facilitates personal transport better than these bicycles can, in these particular environments, seems irrelevant to whether these features make for a better bicycle.

The proponent of the Better Realization Argument, however, might respond by saying that this example is misleading. It does seem sensible that we continue to strive for bicycles that will transport people in these urban environments, despite the greater effectiveness of the car in this regard, but this is due to other factors that provide us with additional reasons to use bicycles in this sub-optimal way. For example, using a bicycle increases physical activity and reduces pollution and energy consumption relative to using a car. Once we bring these factors into the picture, it of course does make sense that we want bicycles to be employed for personal transport, despite their relative inefficiency at this task. But these factors serve to obscure the truth of an important general principle, which is that we ought to use the most efficient means for achieving a given aim, in the absence of any such complicating factors, or, as we might say, "all else being equal." For instance, imagine that we compare bicycling as a means of personal transport with walking. Bicycling is far more efficient and effective as transport. If it were further true that both offered equal health benefits and equal environmental costs, then it would seem that the rational thing to do would be to employ the bicycle for this purpose.[7]

Following this line of thought, we might reconstruct the Better Realization Argument once more, this time spelling out our second premise more carefully and adding a fourth:

1. Design is made expressive in order to display our valuable nature.
2. If Xs have P in order to perform F (and P has no other advantages), but F is done better by something else, then P is not a good-making feature of Xs.
3. The display of our valuable nature is better done by things other than expressive Design objects (namely, actions).
4. There are no other advantages to expression in Design.
5. So, expression is not a good-making feature of Design.

Our additional premise states that there is no, as it were, "spin-off benefit" from using Design objects as the medium of expression or symbolization, in the way that there are spin-off benefits of using the bicycle as a mode of personal transportation.[8]

This way of formulating the Better Realization Argument makes explicit its fundamental idea: that there is something *irrational* about the kind of expression that underlies much of our love of ornament in Design. Modernist views of Design are often charged with over-emphasizing a "Deified Reason," or insisting on an overly rigid and inflexibly rational approach to design (Brolin 1976, 16). This hyper-rationality is a frequent basis for criticisms of Modernist approaches, and is connected by critics to supposed social pathologies of a broader scope, such as capitalism or the obsession with efficiency.

However, the kind of rationality at play in the Better Realization Argument is, as we have seen, of a more humble and familiar kind. It is the use of our available resources in such a way that we have the best likelihood of achieving our aims to the fullest degree possible. This is neither a deification of reason, nor an idea germane to any specific economic system, such as capitalism. The rationality Modernism deploys against ornamentation is no more exaggerated or mysterious than the rationality we deploy in countless mundane tasks of daily life: drinking tea in a teacup, not a bowl; clipping our nails with clippers rather than garden shears; jogging in our Nikes, not our Oxfords.

4.4 Illusion and Reality

Above, we noted that the Better Realization Argument has to be qualified to exclude any compensating benefits that expressive Design might produce. One might argue that we have excluded an obvious benefit here. One might concede that expression is not an optimal means for the aim of displaying a valuable nature, but insist that expression has the benefit of generating the illusion, or the mere perception, of a valuable nature. Material objects may not be the optimal means for conveying the truth about who I am, but they may be very successful in generating an illusion about who I am. And this, it could be argued, is itself a benefit. For such illusions can allow me to be seen by others as the sort of person I would like to be. Also, the widespread use of such illusions would have the general benefit of making the world appear to be a much better place than it is, full of people who are better and more attractive.[9]

This issue emerges not only in cases of expressive ornament applying to persons, but also in cases of expressive ornamentation of buildings and communities (through ornamentation in rituals or ceremonies, for instance). Modernist thinkers were keenly aware of nineteenth-century architecture's widespread use of historical styles, particularly classical ones, to symbolize power, prestige and other ideas. Commercial and civic buildings were lavishly adorned with the forms of Greek and Roman temples, not in the hopes of conveying anything about the nature of the institution, but in the hopes of arousing the respect and prestige associated with the classical world. One might argue that this use of expressive ornament to generate illusions was very effective. If so, then perhaps it is not so irrational, after all, to employ ornament in this way.

What is the Modernist response to this line of thought? In architecture, some critics objected to the crass commercial or political motives behind such illusions. The American sculptor Horatio Greenough derided the "Greek temple jammed in between the brick shops of Wall street or Cornhill, covered with lettered signs, and occupied by groups of money-changers and apple women" (1853, 126). In these cases, one might argue that the supposed benefit of the illusion accrues only to a self-serving elite, insofar as the illusion serves to blind the general populace to their unethical behavior. In modern times, critics have raised similar objections to brands and labels as expressive symbols (see Klein 1999, for example). But this will hardly do as grounds for a general rejection of "illusory expression," for not all illusions need conceal some nefarious behavior. Geoffrey Scott describes the distinction by way of an analogy:

> If, in discharge of a debt, a man were to give me instead of a sovereign a gilded farthing, he would fail, no doubt, of his promise, which was to give me the value of twenty shillings. To deceive me was essential to his plan and the desire to do so implied in his attempt. But if, when I have lent him nothing, he were to give me a gilt farthing because I wanted something bright, and because he could not afford the sovereign at all, then, though the coin might be a false sovereign, there is evidently neither evil will nor injury. There is no failure of promise because no promise has been made. (Scott [1914] 1999, 117–18)

Many cases of expressive design are like Scott's second case: we do not expect the illusion to correspond to reality, and so are not cheated when it fails to do so. What we desire is just the illusion itself.

The discussion here hinges on a deeper philosophical issue: the relation of illusions in general (not merely obviously nefarious ones) to the quality of the lives we lead. The Modernist view seems committed to the notion that the illusions offered by expressive Design are related to our lives in a negative fashion. One idea that could be offered in favor of this is that such illusions serve as a kind of psychological crutch or aid that we use to get along in the world.

The Modernist ideal, on the other hand, calls on us to forgo this reliance on material goods, to see the world for what it is, and to let others see us as we truly are. Along these lines, Loos writes, rather dramatically, that "Freedom from ornament is a sign of spiritual strength" ([1908] 1970, 24). In the spell of the seductive and comforting illusions generated by our possessions, it might be said, we live a sort of half-life. For the better the illusions of myself that I can project, the less *I* need to be better.[10]

It might be objected that this is a strange position for a philosophy of Design to adopt, however. Modernism began, after all, with an embrace of the possibilities of mass production. But it apparently ends by urging us to spurn its products and resist their allures. Something, it might be thought, has gone wrong here. The Modernist might reply, however, that she does not say that the products of Design are worthless, or to be despised: on the contrary, she insists that they are crucial for fulfilling various purposes and functions, and should be well made for those ends. It is only their use in the generation of illusions that ought to be rejected. The Modernist view does manifest a reluctance to give ourselves over to the products of Design too completely, but perhaps it is a wholly uncritical celebration of expression through material objects that would be inappropriate.

But, against the Modernist view, it might still be pointed out that a total exclusion of illusion from our lives, however much it might force us to be strong or self-reliant, would doubtless impoverish our lives in other ways. Many of the fine arts, for example, trade in illusions: fictional scenarios in which we immerse ourselves, as when we lose ourselves in the world of a novel or a film. It is a large question what we get from the experience of engaging with these fictions, but it is generally thought that the experience is a valuable one.[11] A person who never engaged with these fictional illusions would, most of us think, be missing something valuable, however much his engagement with reality might force him to develop himself. Illusion can be a crutch, but it can also be more: it can engage and develop our imaginations, allow us to consider different possibilities for living, and provide us with a version of emotions and experiences that we would not otherwise have. If illusions have these benefits, why exclude them from Design?

To this point, the Modernist has this reply: here again, as in the Better Realization Argument, we have at hand a means for achieving the ends in question that is better than expressive Design, namely the fine arts. One advantage that the fictive arts have over expressive Design is that they are governed by conventions that make the boundaries and status of fiction more or less clear: when the film starts we know that we are in the realm of illusion, and when it ends we know that we are to return to reality. The illusions of expressive Design, on the other hand, permeate our daily lives insofar as Design objects are always around us. Above, I mentioned Scott's idea that, in Design, we do not expect the ideas conveyed to be true, but perhaps this is not quite accurate. It might be more to the point to say that we do not really consider their truth or falsity at all, but simply absorb and, unconsciously, embrace them. The result is an intermingling of these illusions with our beliefs about reality. The arts, by hiving the fictional off from the rest of life, avoid this confusion. Perhaps this is the thought behind comment, in "Ornament and crime," that "anyone who goes to [Beethoven's] *Ninth Symphony* and then sits down and designs a wallpaper pattern is either a confidence trickster or a degenerate" ([1908] 1970, 24). The man who has outgrown ornament has not outgrown illusion, but he knows where and when it belongs.

4.5 An Objection

In this chapter, we have seen the Modernist wield an intuitive rational principle against expression in Design. However, even if we accept the Modernist's arguments, this principle may end up proving too much. As we have noted, even the Modernist does not want to *completely* eliminate the expressive dimension of Design. Good Design, by her lights, will still communicate the *Zeitgeist*, the spirit of the age, through its functional features. But here it seems that the rational principle deployed in the Better Expression Argument can be turned *against* the Modernist's own position. For one might argue that the symbolization of the *Zeitgeist* is, in fact, something done better by certain forms of fine art than by Design: music, perhaps, or long narrative-style art forms such as the novel.

At least one argument can be offered in favor of this view, which is that the expression of broad and complex ideas, like the *Zeitgeist*, in Design objects is severely constrained by practical considerations. For instance, someone Designing a piece of furniture, such as a chair, has to make something that can be sat upon, sold for a certain price and so on. Art, in contrast, escapes from such considerations.[12] Perhaps, then, it is the novel or television series that is the optimal medium for embodying the spirit of the age. If so, then it seems the reasoning of the Better Realization Argument would have bite not only against expressive ornamentation, but against Modernism itself. Should she use the argument to reject ornamentation, the Modernist would be saddled with the unpalatable view that good Design can have no meaning or expressive power whatsoever. The Modernist's reasoning, then, seems to leave her hoisted with her own petard.

The Modernist might get around this objection, however, by emphasizing the idea that the embodiment of the *Zeitgeist* in Design is supposed to be a spin-off, or by-product, of functional construction. If this is true, then in a sense the Modernist view does not require that we irrationally choose to use Design for the expression of the *Zeitgeist*, for we do not choose to do so at all; this merely happens inevitably and naturally. So it might be true that there are other media – certain fine arts, for example – that would provide for a fuller or more satisfying expression of the *Zeitgeist*; nonetheless, the Better Realization Argument would not cut against the Modernist conception of good Design.

This response might seem to rescue the Modernist view from inconsistency, but, even if it does, it puts heavy weight upon the claim that functional Design "automatically" expresses the *Zeitgeist*. Could this claim be true? To find out, we now must turn to investigating more closely the central concept at the heart of the Modernist view: function.

5

The Concept of Function

As we have seen, the Modernist way of thinking addresses the epistemological problem for Design by putting function, in the sense of satisfying practical ends, at its very core: as the slogan goes, form is to follow from function. Modernists have not often elaborated on what exactly they mean by "function," but this might not be thought problematic. At first glance, the notion of function seems intuitive and familiar, and so a reasonable foundation for thinking about Design. It hardly seems like any great insight is needed to know what the function of a chair is, for example. And yet, given the weight placed upon the concept by Modernists, there has been controversy about the very concept of function. Some have even been so appalled by Modernism's uses (or abuses) of the concept, that they have endorsed dropping the notion from discussion of Design altogether. In this chapter, we will identify and explore some of the surprisingly thorny questions raised by the apparently innocent notion of "function."

5.1 The Indeterminacy of Function

A preliminary worry one might have about placing function at the heart of our account of Design is that the term itself has a somewhat artificial quality. When we use or discuss artefacts we do not often use the term "function": we are more likely to talk about what an artefact is for, or what it is supposed to do (Houkes and Vermaas 2010, 46). While this is true, however, the term "function" is widely used in more theoretical discussions of Design. Moreover, the *notion* that arefacts have functions seems to be part of our everyday conceptual framework, even if the word is seldom used, since asking about the function of a given artefact is unlikely to elicit serious puzzlement. Indeed, even a child could identify, if asked, the function of many particular Design objects. This very obviousness and transparency in the notion of function seems to recommend it for the central role that Modernism assigns to it. However, if we look at some other cases, perhaps this appearance of clarity is misleading.

In architecture, for example, there are often heated debates about what exactly the function of a particular building is. Many high-profile architectural projects furnish examples. As a case in point, consider Daniel Libeskind's 2007 renovation of the Royal Ontario Museum. When Libeskind revealed his proposed Design for a new entrance to the museum – a giant, irregularly shaped crystal – some objected on the grounds that it was obviously unsuitable for a building with the function of displaying historical artefacts and art, as the interior's sloping walls made it an awkward display space. Libeskind's defenders, however, replied that the building's main function was not this sort of display, but rather bringing the wider community together in a common space. In light of that, they argued, the striking and dramatic shape of the building was entirely apt (Parsons 2011).

Cases like this one show that, as the philosopher Roger Scruton puts it, "the idea of 'the function' of a building is far from clear" (1979, 40). It is not always so easy to say just what the function of an artefact is: in the above example, both sides seem to have a decent case for their particular view. In these cases, it seems that "the" function of the object cannot be specified: it is "something indeterminate" (40; Parsons and Carlson 2008, 49–57). It might be thought that this indeterminacy is a problem only for complex cases in architecture; surely such indeterminacy does not arise if we consider simpler artefacts, such as our earlier example of a chair. Who could deny that its function is for sitting down? Yet even here the notion of function is, perhaps, not so easy to pin down. If I buy a chair and use it, not for sitting, but to display some books in my living room, or to hang the next day's clothes on before I go to bed, aren't these things the "function" of that artefact? Indeed, we would naturally describe this as a case of a chair functioning as a display stand, or a clothes rack. And if I never actually use my chair for sitting, why privilege sitting down as its function, excluding these other alternatives?

The indeterminacy of function, then, seems to be a real difficulty. And the challenge it presents for the Modernist view is clear: how can the Modernist advise Designers to focus on function, if there is no way to decide what the function of an artefact is? For reasons like these, some have suggested that accounts of Design should simply drop the notion of function altogether. As David Pye bluntly put it, "function is a fantasy" (1978, 12; for similarly pessimistic views see also Scruton 1979; Michl 1995).

However, this wholesale rejection of the concept of function may be an over-reaction. As noted above, talk about function is a common and useful part of the discourse of Design. The problem of indeterminacy does behoove us, however, to provide a *theory of function* that can identify which of the various candidates is an artefact's true function. If such a theory could be provided, then perhaps the Modernist's appeal to function need not put her on shaky ground.

Before we look at some possibilities for such a theory, we must get clearer about the idea of "true function" that this theory is supposed to illuminate. The concept at issue here is more commonly referred to as "proper function": although we may describe a given thing as having various functions, some of these stand apart from the rest as its proper functions (Parsons and Carlson 2008, 65–7).

The term, if not the idea, originated with the philosopher Ruth Millikan (1984, 1989), but it has become generally used in the philosophical literature.[1] The notion can be characterized in different ways: firstly, a proper function is not accidental. The cellphone in your front pocket might deflect a bullet and save your life, but, even if does, that is not its proper function. Secondly, a proper function is not something merely imposed on an object, as when one uses a cellphone as a paperweight. A third way of characterizing proper functions, which is more positive, if metaphorical, is as "belonging to the thing itself": thus we might say that allowing communication is the function that actually belongs to the phone itself, whereas holding down paper does not. We needn't take this talk of "belonging to the object" literally in terms of ontology, but it does point to a distinction that we draw between some functions (the proper ones) and the rest.

A fourth linguistic feature pointing in this same direction is our use of the phrase "function of" as opposed to "function as." So we say that a cell phone has the *function of* communication even if it may *function as* a paperweight (Wright 1973, 141). Proper functions also seem to play an important role in defining types: hence the particular object I have been describing is classified as a cellphone, not a paperweight or bullet deflector. Finally, a crucial part of the concept of proper function is its normativity: proper functions allow for the possibility of malfunction. So if my cellphone cannot make calls, I say it malfunctions, but if it fails to deflect bullets, or is a lousy paperweight, it would be bizarre for me to make any such claim of malfunction. This indicates that, in a sense, doing these things is not really "the item's function."

As I mentioned, proper functions are not the only functions there are. So we could truly say that, in certain circumstances, a cellphone functioned *as* a bullet deflector or a paperweight, and we might want some account of these function ascriptions too. However, most theorists of artefact functions see proper functions as one genuine type of function, and view accounting for their distinctive nature as an important theoretical goal. It shows up, in one way or another, on most lists of desiderata for philosophical theories of artefact function (Preston 2003; Vermaas and Houkes 2003; Houkes and Vermaas 2010, 6–7).

5.2   Intentionalist Theories of Artefact Function

The question, then, is what exactly we mean when we say that X's "real" or proper function is doing this or that.[2] The most intuitive way of accounting for how artefacts obtain their proper functions is in terms of the relation these artefacts have to human intentions. Artefacts are, after all, usually understood as things intentionally made by human beings for some purpose (Hilpinen 2011). So-called "Intentionalist theories" of function understand proper functions in just this way: on this view, an artefact acquires a proper function when, and only when, a certain person has a certain intention that it do something. This "something" becomes its proper function. The most natural way to develop this view is in terms of the intentions that the Designer has toward the artefact he or she Designs. This approach lines up nicely with the picture of Designing that has emerged so far in our discussion: a Designer confronts a practical problem, works out something that will solve it, and that is what the thing in question is for, its proper function.[3]

We can see how this approach would serve to resolve the indeterminacy about function mentioned earlier. In the architectural example, the proper function of Libeskind's ROM extension would be whatever the Designer – Libeskind – intended the building to accomplish. If others have different thoughts or ambitions as to its purpose, or decide to use it in some other way, this would simply be irrelevant insofar as its proper function is concerned. Likewise in our chair example: if the Designer of the chair that I purchased intended it to be used for sitting down, then that is its proper function, whatever I might intend to use it for. It might be true that the chair *functions as* a display stand, or a clothes rack, but it does not have the *function of* doing these various things.

This Intentionalist approach to artefact proper function is very intuitive and attractive.[4] However, it faces a serious objection, which is that the Designer's intentions do not always line up with an artefact's proper function, as the theory implies they should.[5] Consider, for example, artefacts that were originally designed for one purpose but are now employed and made for a different one, such as pipe cleaners (Preston 1998; see also Idhe 2008; Nanay 2010, 412). Originally designed as smoking aids, pipe cleaners are now a material for children's crafts. Similar cases are legion: cellophane, which today has the proper function of covering food, was invented as a tablecloth; Viagra, the famous treatment for erectile dysfunction, was originally designed as a heart medication, and so on.

What these examples show is that the intentions behind a thing's Design are not always sufficient to give it a proper function. An Intentionalist might respond to these counter-examples, however, by shifting to a theory employing not the intentions of the *Designer* of the artefact, but those of the *user*. On this approach, pipe cleaners would have the proper function of serving as a craft material because, even though they were not invented for that reason, people today use them for that purpose (one could argue likewise for cellophane and Viagra). However, this modification of the Intentionalist theory runs up against the fact, mentioned earlier, that many of the things people do with artefacts do not line up with their proper functions. Although I, as a user, may intend my chair to serve as a clothes hanger, this merely allows it to *function as* a clothes hanger, not to have this as its function. This point becomes clearer when we reflect on all the unusual and idiosyncratic ways in which people use arte-facts: wielding a frying pan as a weapon, using a bike pump as a door stop, and so on. As a last resort, the Intentionalist might rework her theory so as to appeal to the intentions not of the Designers or users of artefacts, but those of their makers or manu-facturers. Yet this theory also fails, for similar reasons, since the people who make artefacts can also do so for reasons that fail to line up with their proper functions. Imagine a man who buys the parts for and assembles a shovel with the intention that it mark the loca-tion of a particular flower in his garden (Parsons 2011). Here again we would have a case of something (a shovel) *functioning as* a garden marker, but not having this as its proper function.

The upshot of this line of argument is that the Intentionalist cannot account for artefact proper function by appealing to the intentions of any specific individual, be that person Designer, maker or user. If she wishes to provide such an account, then, she must specify a particular *kind* of intention that is sufficient for giving something a proper function, whomever should happen to have it. For example, one might suggest that intentions bestow proper func-tions on artefacts only when they are sufficiently creative, or involve modifying the structure of the object in some interesting way. This could allow us to explain why using a chair as a clothes rack or a doorstop does not give it those proper functions. Preston (2003), however, argues persuasively that there is no obvious way that the Intentionalist can specify an intention of the right kind. She notes that many of the idiosyncratic things that users do with artefacts are very creative, and involve modifying the artefact (making a frying pan into a satellite dish, for example). Yet these uses, and the intentions behind them, do not suffice to bestow a proper function upon the artefact.

Perhaps, however, the Intentionalist can try a slightly different approach. Houkes and Vermaas (2010) suggest construing the sort of intention that generates proper function, not in terms of its intrinsic qualities, but rather in terms of its relation to social con-ventions and attitudes. In developing this view, they first distinguish between proper and improper use of artefacts: "Proper use" they write, "is the execution of a use plan that is accepted within a certain community; improper use is the execution of a use plan that is socially disapproved" (93). For Houkes and Vermaas, a use plan is a certain kind of complex intention about how an artefact is to be used, what is to be done with it and so on. They then define "proper function ascriptions as function ascriptions, by designers, justifiers and passive users, relative to proper use plans" (93). So, on this view, a function is not a proper function if it is not part of a socially approved way of using the artefact in question. Thus, using a frying pan as a weapon would not count as a proper function of that kind of artefact, since using it in this way is part of a use plan that lacks social approval. Using it for cooking, on the other hand, is a part of a use plan that is "accepted within a certain community." "In this way," Houkes and Vermaas write, "our philosophy of artefacts accommodates the proper–accidental desideratum" for theories of artefact function (2010, 93).

However, it is not so clear that the notions of social approval and disapproval will do the work that Houkes and Vermaas want them to do: much depends upon how these notions are to be understood. In cases like using a frying pan as a weapon, it is clearly true that this use is subject to social disapproval, insofar as using weapons is generally (though of course not universally) frowned on. But is this true for other cases of non-proper functions? Think of some of our earlier examples: using a frying pan as a satellite dish, or using a shovel as a garden marker. These are odd intentions, to be sure, but they would hardly be subject to "social disapproval" in any meaningful sense. Moreover, it is not clear that all proper functions require social approval: consider sex toys. In conservative cultures, sex toys face enormous social disapproval. Yet that fact does not make it the case that those artefacts merely "function as" sex toys: rather, they *are* sex toys. This suggests that social approval and disapproval is really irrelevant to the proper/non-proper function distinction.

There is another way of interpreting the notions of social approval and disapproval, however. One could say that using a frying pan for cooking and using a shovel for digging are socially accepted, whereas using a frying pan as a weapon and a shovel as a garden stake are not, if we understand "social acceptance" to mean something more like "already established as a common practice." In the case of sex toys also, we might say that their sexual use is their proper function since that is what people actually do with them. This reinterpretation, however, represents a fundamental shift away from the Intentionalist theory of proper function: no longer is it human plans, intentions or attitudes that determine an artefact's proper function. Instead, something further is required: an actual established kind of use of the artefact type in question. With this move we leave the Intentionalist approach behind, and adopt a distinct theory of proper function, one appealing to an item's history.

5.3 Evolutionary Theories of Artefact Function

If an appeal to human intentions will not allow us to draw the distinction between accidental and proper functions for artefacts, then we must move beyond the realm of intention in formulating a theory of artefact function. The most prominent theory of this sort is the so-called "evolutionary" or "etiological" theory of artefact function.[6] This theory is inspired by an account of functions in the biological realm. It is natural for both laymen and scientists to talk about the functions of animal parts and traits, as when we speak of the heart's function being to pump blood, or birds' wings as having the function of facilitating flight. Furthermore, these functions seem to be proper functions, which can be contrasted with functions of the parts or traits that are merely accidental (e.g., the heart's functioning as a noise maker). In such cases, however, we clearly cannot appeal to human intentions as the basis of these functions. A more appealing option is to look to the role played by these functional effects in the causal history (or etiology) of the sort of trait or part involved. Thus, we might say, for example, that pumping blood is the heart's proper function, whereas making noise is not, because the former, but not the latter, played a role in the history of reproduction of that sort of organ. Put another way, current hearts exist, in part, because of their ability to pump blood, but not because of their noise-making capacity (Godfrey-Smith 1994). We can adapt this view to provide a theory of artefact function in the following way: "X has a *proper function* F if and only if Xs currently exist because, in the recent past, ancestors of X were successful in meeting some need or want in the marketplace because they performed F, leading to manufacture and distribution of Xs."[7] The key idea that this theory takes up from the biological case is what Preston describes as "a history of reproduction contingent upon success" (1998, 244). So, in the case of something like a stapler, we could say that its proper function is to allow the quick binding of paper because it is *that* effect, rather than its other effects (taking up space, holding papers down, causing injuries, for example) which has caused new tokens of the type to be produced, by satisfying a want or need in the marketplace – the need to quickly bind loose papers.[8]

It is important to note that, on this account, it isn't necessarily a process of *selection* that generates proper function.[9] In the biological case, one way to develop an evolutionary theory of function would be to propose that traits acquire their proper functions when something that they do allows organisms bearing them to outcompete organisms with variant traits, resulting in natural selection of the trait. Thus, we might say that bird feathers have the proper function of facilitating flight because they allowed birds with them to leave more offspring than their featherless rivals. In the case of artefacts, a selection-based account of proper function is somewhat more complicated, as the selection occurs through intentional processes of making and purchasing rather than purely natural ones. However, we might construe the evolutionary theory for artefacts in this same general way, taking proper functions to be effects that allow one variant of an artefact to outcompete its rivals, thereby being "selected."

However, selection-based accounts of proper function are problematic, in both the biological and artefactual cases (see Schwartz 1999; Preston 2013). One problem is that the evolution of biological traits is not always explained by the operation of natural selection. It may be, for example, that no variation in the trait was present, and in this circumstance natural selection cannot occur. Or a trait may be present in a population simply through genetic drift, as when the trait comes to be reproduced simply because variants happened to die off due to chance events (natural disasters, disease and so on). In these cases, a theory that identifies proper functions with effects that are naturally selected over rivals will be unable to attribute a proper function. However, if we discovered that bird feathers originally evolved due to genetic drift rather than selective success, it seems we would still want to say that facilitating flight is their proper function.

As Preston (2009) points out, this same issue is, if anything, an even more significant problem for a selection-based evolutionary theory of proper function in artefacts. Many artefacts do not even exist in significantly different variant forms (Preston offers the example of silverware, which displays minimal stylistic variation).

When there *are* differing variants of an artefact type, it is often the case that one variant outcompetes the others not because it does a better job of satisfying wants and needs, but because of random, external reasons, such as poor advertising on the part of its rivals, economic considerations or a near-monopoly held by its manufacturers. In the 1980s, VHS video recorders outperformed Beta format recorders, not because they allowed for better playback, but for economic reasons. Although it was widely agreed that Beta format players were superior to VHS, they never sold well and eventually vanished. Marking the analogy with the biological case of evolution by genetic drift, Preston refers to this phenomenon as "cultural drift."

However, these limitations of the idea of selection need not spell disaster for the evolutionary theory. For that theory does not require a proper function to have caused the item in question to be *selected* over its rivals: it only requires it to have contributed to the reproduction of the item type. In the biological case, it may do so by enhancing the organism's fitness (Buller 1998). So, even if they originated due to genetic drift, feathers still seem to have a fitness-enhancing effect by facilitating flight: this seems to explain birds' ability to survive and reproduce. In the artefact case, an effect may do something analogous to enhancing fitness by facilitating the ability to meet needs and wants in the marketplace. So even if playing recorded video images did not allow the VHS recorder to achieve selective success over its rivals, we can still say that this is its proper function if this effect explains why VCRs were reproduced, which it does seem to do. Hence it would count as its proper function (Preston 1998; Parsons and Carlson 2008).

A second point to note about the evolutionary theory is that it makes the proper function of artefacts a matter to be determined through empirical investigation. One aspect of this point is that some artefacts may turn out to have multiple proper functions, if they do multiple things that lead to the reproduction of their type. A deeper aspect is that it is logically possible, as far as this account goes, that an artefact, or even all artefacts, have *no* proper function at all. This would occur if a type of thing was reproduced purely randomly or arbitrarily rather than because it satisfies some need or want. Of course, this seems not at all plausible for actual artefacts: the reproduction of an artefact type takes resources, time and effort, and does not offer the incentive of carnal pleasure, as biological reproduction does. But it isn't a logical impossibility: we can imagine a race of people who arbitrarily make random things for no good reason.

This point reveals that the evolutionary theory relies on an empirical principle that we could call "No reproduction without utility." The idea behind this principle is, in Preston's words, that "reproduction in the face of consistent failure would be arbitrary or irrational" (2013, 179). People *could* behave this way, but we don't believe that, in general, real people do. The kind of rationality at play here, it should be noted, is compatible with the sorts of "external factors" at play in the aforementioned cases of cultural drift. It may be that VHS recorders did not triumph because of their superiority in satisfying market demands. Despite that, there must still be *something* that they did successfully; otherwise (according to our principle) they would not have been reproduced.

A third and final point about this theory is that the successful effects that it identifies with proper functions have to be *real* effects. This is perhaps most evident in the biological case: if a proper function is the reason that a type of trait is reproduced, then the proper function must be a real effect. For example, if facilitating flight is the proper function of wings then wings must actually facilitate flight. Translated to the artefact case, the salient point is that proper functions cannot be merely *perceived* successes. People might believe, for example, that a certain kind of drug helps to cure a disease, but unless it actually does, this effect (curing the disease) cannot explain its reproduction and so cannot be its proper function. Of course, such a drug might have the very real effect of *causing people to believe that they are treating the disease* (this is the so-called "placebo effect"), and we might identify the proper function of the drug as doing that (that is, we might consider it a placebo). However, this is a distinct effect from curing the disease. In general, then, we might say this theory of proper function ties proper functions to what is really the case.

It is also important to see that embracing an evolutionary theory of artefact function does not entail entirely rejecting the Intentionalist view described in the previous section. Although some proponents of the etiological theory do reject any Intentionalist view of function, it is entirely possible to combine the two views, holding that, while intentions can bestow functions upon artefacts, it is only causal history that can bestow proper function.[10] The idea behind such a "pluralist" theory of functions can perhaps be more clearly seen when put in terms of function ascriptions: intentions that an artefact do X, on the part of a user or manufacturer, for example, are what justify us in saying that the object *functions as* an X, but only the artefact's causal history can justify us in saying that it *has the function of* doing X.

The main point in favor of the evolutionary theory, then, is that it seems to resolve the worry, raised at the start of this chapter, about the indeterminacy of function. If we want to know the proper function of an artefact, we look to its causal history to see which of its effects played a causal role in the reproduction of its ancestors. Thus, in the more vexed case of our architectural example, the proper function of Libeskind's museum expansion would be to do whatever it is that, in the recent past, has led buildings of that sort to be produced (see Parsons 2011).

5.4 Objections to the Evolutionary Theory

The evolutionary theory is hardly free from criticism, however. In this section, I examine some of the key objections to it. One difficulty concerns the way in which the theory specifies the relevant causal history for any given type of artefact. Parsons and Carlson (2008), for example, refer to the success of the artefact's "ancestors." But artefacts do not have ancestors in the straightforward, literal sense in which organisms do, since artefacts do not reproduce themselves. Rather, they must be produced intentionally by people. But then how are we to understand the idea that one artefact is to be viewed as the "ancestor" of another?

One account of "ancestry" for the evolutionary theory is given by Millikan (1984). Millikan defines the notion of an ancestor in relation to what she calls a "reproductively established family." A reproductively established family is a group of things that all share a certain character, or similar character, and which possess that character because they were all copied, directly or indirectly, from the same model. Copying, in Millikan's sense, need not be done intentionally (although it can be): the key idea is that copying involves what philosophers call "counterfactual dependence" between the characters of the things involved. Counterfactual dependence is the idea that one thing depends on another thing in the sense that, had the first thing been different, so would the second. With respect to copying, the idea is that the character of one thing is a copy of another thing just in case, had the first thing lacked that character, so would the second thing. For Millikan, then, a reproductively established family is a group of things whose shared characteristic is generated by this kind of copying. Millikan applies this to artefacts, such as common household screwdrivers. They are all part of a reproductively established family, since they have a certain character – a similar shape, size, weight, etc. – that has been copied from the same model. Millikan then defines the notion of an ancestor using the notion of such a family. The ancestors of my screwdriver, for example, will be those prior members of the family from which its character was copied.[11]

Whether or not the notion of an ancestor can be adequately defined, there are two deeper problems facing the evolutionary theory. The first of these is the phenomenon of "phantom functions." "Phantom functions," in Preston's words, "are cases where an item of material culture is constitutionally incapable of performing a function it is widely taken to have" (Preston 2013, 177). And yet, she maintains, these functions "have all the earmarks of proper functions" (177). Preston offers numerous examples, such as communion wafers, whose proper function seems to be allowing the consumption of Christ's body; rabbit's-foot charms, whose proper function seems to be to give one good luck; and (perhaps more controversially) vitamin C supplements, whose proper function is warding off disease. Her favorite example, however, is that of the *feng shui* mirror, whose proper function is apparently directing the flow of a spiritual substance known in Chinese folklore as *qi*. These "*ba gua* mirrors" are placed in certain locations outside the home so as to direct negative *qi* away, in order to keep the home spiritually healthy.

Since none of the things just mentioned can actually do the thing that is apparently its proper function, these are all examples of phantom functions. The problem they pose for the evolutionary theory should be clear: as discussed in the previous section, proper functions, on the evolutionary theory, must be real effects, but phantom functions are not. So if phantom functions can be proper functions, then the evolutionary theory is false.

The defender of the evolutionary theory might respond to this objection by insisting that these prima facie identifications of phantom functions as proper functions are simply mistaken. They might then appeal to other effects of the artefacts in question which, unlike the phantom functions, can in fact explain the reproduction of the artefact type.[12] In the case of *feng shui* mirrors, one might look to anthropological or sociological accounts of *feng shui* for such an explanation. For example, one might suggest that the reason these artefacts have been reproduced is not that they deflect *qi* but that they satisfy a psychological need, such as allowing practitioners to feel that their homes are healthy places, or a need for hope and security (Wang et al. 2013).

Preston objects to this strategy for identifying proper functions, however, on the grounds that the explanations invoked are overly generic. She offers the example of something's being a commodity: a social scientist might explain the reproduction of phantom function items – *feng shui* mirrors, for example – by referring to their use as commodities. She writes:

> Being a commodity . . . is certainly a role items of material culture play in certain kinds of economies. But in those economies pretty much everything is in principle a commodity. . . . So it does not seem appropriate to say this is the specific proper function of any of them. The commodities that are items of material culture do have proper functions, but connected with their specific uses, not to their generic exchangeability. (2013, 184)

Preston is surely right to insist that any decent explanation we give of the reproduction of some artefact type should pertain to the "specific uses" of that sort of artefact. However, the general claim that social science explanations for the reproduction of artefact types must fail to account for their specific uses seems false.[13] Take the claim, mentioned earlier, that *feng shui* mirrors are reproduced to allow practitioners to sustain hope in the face of uncertainty and chance. This by no means need apply to "pretty much every-thing . . . in principle": there is no reason to think that toasters or urinals are made because of this, and some artefacts are reproduced for the opposite reason (think of thrill rides such as rollercoasters, for example). More to the point, such an explanation can be specific in the sense of tying into and explaining specific patterns of use: so we might say, for example, that people buy *feng shui* mirrors and put them over their doors, because this fosters hope *by allowing practitioners to feel that their home is healthy*.[14] In any case, it is plain that many other objects do not foster hope in the same way, and in this sense the explanation can be entirely specific to the particular patterns of use that pertain to *feng shui* mirrors.

But even if we grant the evolutionary theorist this response to the case of phantom functions, there remains a deeper problem for her theory. This is the fact that the evolutionary theory is unable to ascribe any proper function to novel artefacts. Since the theory makes having a proper function a matter of an artefact's reproductive history, an artefact that lacks any such history – a novel artefact – cannot have such a function. In the case of the phantom function objection discussed above, the evolutionary theorist can respond to the objection by looking to other effects that the artefact's ancestors might have had, which could explain reproduction of the artefact type. But in this case, no such response is possible, since the artefact in question simply has no ancestors at all. Here, an explanation of the right sort is not merely elusive, it is impossible.

Some have argued that the conclusion that novel artefacts cannot have proper functions is deeply counterintuitive, and constitutes grounds for rejecting the evolutionary theory.[15] Vermaas and Houkes, for example, see allowing the ascription of proper functions to novel artefacts as a requirement for any satisfactory theory of artefact function (2003, 266; Houkes and Vermaas 2010). They also stress the particular importance of novelty and innovation from the perspective of Design: novel prototypes seem to be vital in Design (2010, 75), and they offer many cases of highly innovative Designs, such as the Brittannia Bridge, a novel bridge Design implemented in Wales in the mid nineteenth century; the first teletype machine (Vermaas and Houkes 2003, 264); the first airplane; and the first nuclear power plant (Houkes and Vermaas 2010, 63–4). They argue that these artefacts were novel at the time of their creation, and, hence, cannot have proper functions, according to the evolutionary theory.

There are two possible responses the defender of the evolutionary theory can make to the problem of novel artefacts. The first is to accept that the theory denies proper function to novel artefacts, but maintain that this is not a fatal flaw. This approach is taken by Preston, who argues that *no* theory can both ascribe proper functions to novel artefacts, *and* draw the distinction between proper and accidental functions (2003). Since, in Preston's eyes, doing the latter is more important than the former, she argues that we still have reason to favor the evolutionary theory over its rivals.[16]

A second possible reply would be to deny that there are, in fact, any truly innovative or novel artefacts – that is, artefacts that lack ancestors. In support of this, it could be argued that many of the putative examples of such artefacts are not so compelling. The Britannia Bridge, for example, had many of the features of previous bridges, and the teletype machine copied many of the features of telegraphs. The first airplane copied many features from previously existing kites, and the first nuclear power plant employed the same basic mechanisms used in previous types of power plants (such as the use of steam) (Parsons and Carlson 2008).[17] If this is the case, then perhaps the evolutionary theory can assign proper functions even to these artefacts.

In response to this, however, it could be insisted that, even if there actually are no novel artefacts, there *could* be, in principle, and it is still a failing of the evolutionary theory that it cannot account for their proper functions (Houkes and Vermaas 2003). However, the evolutionary theorist might respond that if the artefact in question is *truly* novel, employing a hitherto *completely* unknown Design, then our intuition that it in fact has a *proper* function at all may become suspect (for an argument along these lines, see Parsons and Carlson 2008).

5.5 Novelty, Design and the Epistemological Problem

In the past several sections, we have been examining some leading theories of artefact function as a way of trying to resist the skeptical idea that the notion of function, which Modernists place at the center of their account of Design, is in fact so obscure that it should be discarded altogether. If the line of thought developed here is cogent, perhaps the evolutionary theory succeeds in this ambition. An evolutionary account of function might also seem to lend some support to the Modernist idea that functional Design will be, *ipso facto*, expressive of a culture's *Zeitgeist*. For if proper function is a matter of the history of use of a particular type of item, then, by its nature, it bears on an aspect of culture. Much more needs to be said, but this conceptual connection at least seems promising for the Modernist. However, this defense of the concept of function also suggests a more profound conclusion – a way of entirely dissolving the epistemological problem for Design.

In chapter 1, we emphasized the way in which Design apparently differs from tradition-based craft in creating *novel* artefacts to solve new, hitherto unaddressed problems. On this view, the Designer emerges as something of a heroic individual, breaking with tradition and attempting something *new*. Recall Christopher Alexander's remark that "the designer . . . stands alone." Furthermore, it was precisely this novelty that gave rise to the epistemological problem for Design: it is because the Designer produces something fundamentally new and untested that the rationality of his creative act is thrown into question. But our investigation of function in this chapter has suggested a rather different picture: that in fact the Designer does *not* create novel artefacts after all, but rather tinkers with and adapts already existing artefact types. This alternative view seems to suggest that Design is as much bound up with the past as tradition-based craft was, and that the epistemological problem for Design is, perhaps, merely an illusion generated by a misconception of the very nature of Design itself.

One source of this error, perhaps, is the tendency, which we earlier saw lamented by Gropius, to conceive of Design too much on the model of the fine arts, which historically have emphasized novelty, uniqueness and originality. Since the emergence of the Romantic movement, the fine arts have emphasized the artist's individuality and seen the artwork as expressive of the individual vision, experience or emotion of the artist. When we think about Design from the Designer's perspective, in terms of the attempt to solve some new problem, there appears to be a strong parallel between the two creative enterprises. But when viewed from the other end, as it were – that is, in terms of the object and its function – we see that Design objects, unlike artworks, are not the unique progeny of individual minds. For the central feature of a Design artefact – its proper function – is not something determined by the individual Designer, but a social aspect of an already-existing artefact type that has evolved through its use and reproduction.

But does this mean that the epistemological problem for Design was merely an illusion? While it is true that our earlier portrait of Design, emphasizing novelty and individual effort at problem solving, left out an important truth about Design, in another sense it was not wholly inaccurate. It may be true, as our discussion of the evolutionary theory suggests, that Designers employ already-existing artefact types, tinkering with them or modifying them. This, it might be thought, gives them access to some knowledge about those types: for example, when the Wright brothers invented the airplane they could draw upon an established body of empirical knowledge about the properties of kites. But when Designers tinker with existing types, they tinker with them or modify them for use in novel contexts, or to do *new things*. And in Design, these contexts are inherently social – they involve not merely practical considerations but considerations of aesthetics, expression and so forth. For these reasons, even if the artefact the Designer creates is not truly novel, the novelty that he or she confronts in the Design problem is real enough, and generates the epistemological difficulties discussed in chapter 2.[18]

Although recognizing the sense in which Design relies upon the past does not eliminate the epistemological problem, it does clarify our understanding of Design itself and in particular the relation between art and Design. In chapter 1, we remarked that Design is "shackled," relative to the fine arts, in the sense that it is subject to the requirement that it solve "real-world" problems. But now we see a second way in which the Designer's task is more arduous than that of the artist. For if Design is art shackled, it is also art inglorious, in the sense that, unlike the artist, the Designer can lay no claim to his creation once it leaves his hand; its nature outstrips him, and in most cases his name is forgotten. Artworks have sometimes been compared to an artist's offspring (Collingwood 1938; Croce 1922). But this analogy is far more apt in the case of a Designer than of the artist. For whereas the artist's works retain their connection with their creator, the "progeny" of the Designer, like real children, must leave their creators behind and make their way in the world on their own. In this sense, Design offers not only greater challenges than art, but also less reward.

6

Function, Form and Aesthetics

So far, we have examined some of the key moves in Modernism: curtailing expression in Design, and putting function to the fore. But beauty, or aesthetic value, also seems to be an important aspect of Design problems. The Modernist concurs that good Design must be aesthetically appealing, but holds that beauty or aesthetic value is to be cultivated simply though the pursuit of functionality, rather than through the use of decoration or a period or cultural style. However, this crucial idea – that when "Form follows Function" the result will be beauty – has been hotly disputed within Design and architecture. Moreover, in philosophical discussions of beauty and aesthetic value the very idea of any connection between beauty and functionality has long been a vexed notion. In this chapter, I explore these and other issues surrounding the aesthetics of Design artefacts.

6.1 Can Form Follow Function?

The Modernist notion is that we can cultivate beauty through the pursuit of functionality. One difficulty for this idea involves the relation between function and form. According to the Modernist view, aesthetic, mediating and expressive aspects need not be brought into the Design problem: it is a purely functional one. Creating the Design object along these purely functional lines will, it is said, give it beauty. But this implies that consideration of function alone is enough to determine a solution to a Design problem: that in Design, as the slogan goes, "Form follows Function."

However, it has been objected that functional considerations alone are not enough to determine form. Another way to put the point is to say that an object's form cannot simply follow from its function: rather, its function always *underdetermines* its form.

This objection is sometimes put forth in a way that emphasizes the particular historical origins of Modernist thinking, and in particular its roots in the so-called "Machine Age" of the late nineteenth century. Many early Modernists were inspired by the industrial machinery of the nineteenth century, such as the locomotive, in which, it seemed, the Design had been determined entirely by functional considerations, each part being present only because it was needed to make the mechanism work, and having its particular form in virtue of its contribution to that end. But the attempt to extend this idea, which arises naturally in the case of industrial machinery, to other Design goods ran into difficulties. The Design historian Penny Sparke describes how:

> As a set of constructional principles the machine aesthetic, and the theory of functionalism, were more easily and appropriately applied to a simple wooden chair or a silver teapot than to a vacuum cleaner or a radio, which ended up necessarily concealing, rather than revealing, their inner structural components. The body-shell principle of the car stylists and the commercial industrial designers, used to conceal inner workings and present a visual illusion of simplicity, proved much more appropriate in the end however much it negated functionalist principles. (2004, 89)

Sparke points to a fundamental difficulty for the idea that function alone can determine a Design's form. In the case of some objects, there is no gap, as it were, between the functional elements of the object and what we might naturally call its form – its outer surface. This is notably the case for machines like the locomotives, where the mechanism's parts are exposed, and also in simple everyday objects like a chair or a teapot. Here the functional elements are not concealed by an outer layer: the object's functionality is manifest entirely in its outer, tangible structure. In other sorts of Design object, however, there is a gap between functionality and form. In the case of a radio, the functional elements are the electronic components which are hidden inside an outer shell, which can take any shape at all without affecting the object's functionality (a more extreme example of the same phenomenon is the variety of objects that can take digital pictures). Indeed, with the rise of consumer electronics, this sort of case is now arguably at least as common as the former case. But in these cases, we see the failure of the idea that function determines form.

However, when presented in this way, the Modernist has a potential reply to this worry. Recall that, in chapter 1, we characterized Design as being distinct from engineering in focusing on the "surface" or "user interface" of things. If this holds true, then the electronic guts of radios and vacuums are not the Designer's concern at all. The functionality that concerns them is, rather, the employment of the object by the user to carry out some task. This aspect of the object's functionality, one could argue, *is* manifest in the objects' "outer shell": in how easily it can be manipulated, how safely it can be used, and so on.

Worries about the relation of function and form are not so easily sidestepped, however. David Pye raises one such worry in a much more general way than Sparke. "When *any useful thing* is designed," Pye writes, "the shape of it is in no way imposed on the designer, or determined by any influence outside him, or entailed" (Pye 1978, 14; emphasis added). Pye's claim is simply that, whenever Designers set out to create something that will perform a given function, they have a wide scope of choice in deciding what form the object should have. The limitations faced by the Designer, Pye says, "arise only in small part from the physical nature of the world, but in a very large measure from considerations of economy and choice" (14). To support this general claim, Pye offers the simple example of ceilings: ceilings are always flat, but to perform their function (presumably that of covering electrical and plumbing components and insulation) they don't *need* to be flat – they could be uneven, and yet do the job equally well (13). A good deal of work, Pye observes, goes into producing this particular form – a flat ceiling – and it is, from the strictly functional point of view, completely "useless work."[1]

Pye offers only one example to support his claim, and perhaps the Modernist would reply that concealing pipes and so forth is a bit of unnecessary decoration anyway (indeed, many Modernist buildings contrive to leave such elements exposed). However, it seems easy to multiply examples of the same sort. For instance, there are apparently innumerable forms that will satisfy, equally well, the function of allowing someone to sit down, as witnessed by the sheer variety of shapes of chairs. The same observation can be extended to countless other Design goods as well: coffee pots, silverware, even doors could be shapes other than they typically are and still serve their purpose.

Pye's claim is thus quite a bit stronger than Sparke's: it is not only goods with a shell that falsify the dictum "Form follows Function," but apparently all goods. Is this claim true? Against Pye's claim, we might argue that it isn't logically or even physically *impossible* for function to determine form. Pye himself mentions propulsive machines (1978, 30), which might furnish an example. In the construction of devices that must penetrate fluids or face air resistance, such as a ship's hull, physical forces constrain functionality so severely that they serve to determine an optimal form. As every swimmer knows, any departure from a streamlined shape in the water results in costly drag. Even if there are such cases, however, it still seems true that *most* cases of the function/form relationship are *not* of this sort: there simply are no forces analogous to the resistance exerted by fluids that could determine, for example, that ceilings must be flat rather than some other shape in order to fulfill their function.

One might try to deny this, by suggesting that such constraining forces do exist generally (see, e.g., Alexander and Poyner 1970). In the case of something like a chair, for example, one might appeal to the sorts of principles concerning utility mentioned in section 2.6. Perhaps there are principles of ergonomics to which we could appeal so as to rule out various Designs as sub-optimal. But even if this is the case, it seems plausible to think that there will still be many equally valid ways of realizing the function of the object using different forms. And even if there *were* only one physical shape, say, that was optimal for realizing the function of a chair, there would still be elements of the object's form that are left undetermined – color being the most obvious of these.[2] The Designer can decide on these elements on the basis of aesthetics, whim, cost or some combination thereof, but he will not have them determined simply by the function of his product.

6.2 Squaring Function and Aesthetic Value

The under-determination of form by function no doubt complicates the picture for the Modernist. However, perhaps the view that beauty can be realized through the pursuit of functionality can still be maintained: perhaps Designs that are functional will thereby have beauty, even though more than functionality must go into their creation. However, this Modernist view, and indeed any discussion of the beauty or aesthetics of Design, immediately runs head-on into a large philosophical question: what *is* beauty, or aesthetic value?[3] We have been assuming that it makes sense to speak of function in connection with beauty, but, as we shall see, this is not a trivial assumption.

In common thought we can identify two main ideas about beauty. Interestingly, these are contradictory: beauty is indefinable, and beauty consists in certain specific characteristics. The latter notion is evident in discussions of the role of geometrical proportions in defining the beauty of the human body, particularly the face (Zebrovitz 1997, 123–4). Thus, some have tried to define beauty in terms of simple mathematical rules, such as the so-called "golden section." On the other hand, we often find beauty written off as a mere personal preference, or a mystery, consisting in a "je ne sais quoi." Although contradictory, these two ideas are related to each other, in the sense that if one tries to extend the idea that beauty consists in a specific mathematical quality very far, it quickly becomes evident that it is false: we call many things beautiful, or aesthetically good, that cannot be understood in these terms (a performance of Macbeth, a symphony and so on). It is then natural to conclude that, after all, beauty must be ineffable.[4]

There is, however, another way to understand the notion, which stands somewhere between these two poles: in terms of a special way of engaging with the world. On this approach, beauty is not a specific quality in things, nor is it indefinable; rather it is what results when we approach the world in a specific way, or, as Jerome Stolnitz puts it, using a specific attitude – the "aesthetic attitude" (Stolnitz 1960). Historically, this idea has been developed mainly in terms of the key notion of distinterestedness. "Disinterestedness" refers not to a lack of interest in something, but to a particular way of approaching it, so that one's response to the thing is not determined by its advancing, or failing to advance, one's interests. Rather, the idea is that one attends to the object without any concern for its relation to one's practical goals, moral standards and so on. To appreciate an object aesthetically, on this view, is to appreciate it in this disinterested manner, engaging with it in isolation from these other factors, and "taking in," as it were, the whole object.

This account takes the aesthetic to be something *subjective* in nature, in the sense that what makes a particular response aesthetic has entirely to do with the subject or appreciator, rather than the thing appreciated. This does not mean that any response at all can be considered aesthetic: it is essential, for Stolnitz, that the subject be disinterested. It also does not entail that there cannot be correct or incorrect judgements about aesthetic value (this is a separate issue that we will take up in section 6.3, below). It does mean, however, that we can take the aesthetic attitude to, as Stolnitz says, "any object of awareness whatever" (1960, 39). This seems to make the aesthetic attitude view promising as a way of understanding the aesthetics of Design, since it does not restrict our aesthetic experiences to the realm of art.

However, this appearance is deceiving, since it turns out to be difficult to adopt the disinterested attitude toward Design objects. In his account, Stolnitz contrasts the aesthetic attitude with what he calls the practical attitude, in which we attend to things for the sake of achieving some ulterior purpose. But when we engage with Design objects, it seems to be precisely the practical attitude that we employ, for they are things that we use in daily life, and so we typically relate to them in terms of our practical goals. It would seem that taking the aesthetic attitude toward a Design object would require taking it out of its usual context and putting it into a very different one.[5] And indeed, Design objects are sometimes exhibited in galleries and museums, in the way that artworks are: in these circumstances, it would seem much easier to take the aesthetic attitude to them, since they are removed from our practical aims. But, one might object, this is an entirely artificial way to regard them. Assessing the aesthetic value of Design this way would be something like judging the character of a person based only on their performances in a play or a film: it is not quite the real person that we are judging.

For this reason, it might be thought that the aesthetic attitude theory, rather than being hospitable to Design, threatens to make the aesthetic appreciation of Design objects flatly impossible. Be that as it may, the theory has in any case been widely criticized. George Dickie (1964), for example, criticized Stolnitz's account on the grounds that the concept of distinterestedness does not pick out a special kind of attention, but refers only to our *motivations* for attending to something. So, to say that I am disinterested does not say anything about *how* I am attending to the object but only about my reasons for doing so. Seen this way, Dickie argues, the concept of disinterestedness becomes irrelevant: if I have a moral or practical motive, my attention to the object can be just as complete as that of a disinterested person who lacks such a motive. Dickie concludes that the whole theory of the "aesthetic attitude" is a confused, and confusing, attempt to say something much simpler, which is that, in appreciating the object, we must pay attention to it and not be distracted by anything else.

Dickie's critique convinced many philosophers to abandon the aesthetic attitude theory. But if we follow this path, the prospects of a satisfying account of the aesthetics of Design do not appear to brighten. On Dickie's account, the notion of distinterestedness drops out of sight, and we are left with the idea that aesthetically appreciating an object involves paying attention to its qualities. But the question immediately arises: which qualities? Take an artwork such as a painting, for example. It has many qualities: its surface is colored, it depicts a woman, it weighs 5 pounds, it is worth a certain sum of money and so on. Intuitively, we want to say that aesthetic appreciation involves attending to the first two qualities, but not the latter two. But why is this? To address this problem, Dickie answers that the qualities that are relevant to aesthetic appreciation are determined by conventions of the artworld (1974, 1984). Whatever the merits of Dickie's account for art, it is apparent that applying this model of the aesthetic to Design will be problematic indeed, since the conventions of the artworld do not tell us what to appreciate in Design, nor is there an analogous "Designworld" to which we might appeal. One could insist that the relevant artworld conventions are to be extended to Design objects, but then we are back to the worry, expressed above, of appreciating Design in an entirely artificial way.

Another prominent alternative to Stolnitz's theory of the aesthetic centers on the notion of aesthetic *experience*. On this view, the term "aesthetic" refers not to a special attitude that we take to things, but to a special sort of experience that we obtain from certain things. Things that provide this kind of experience are said to be aesthetically good. A sophisticated version of this theory was developed, with great subtlety, by the philosopher Monroe Beardsley, who characterized aesthetic experience as intense, unified and complex (1958). Beardsley's view provides a compelling account of the aesthetics of much art, but, as he himself came to see, it fails to illuminate our transient encounters with things (Beardsley 1982). In this regard, it is as inhospitable to Design as Stolnitz's account, since we typically engage with Design objects in a transient way.

This persistent incompatibility between Design and theories of the aesthetic has prompted some philosophers interested in the aesthetics of Design to look for a new concept of the aesthetic altogether. Arto Haapala, for example, proposes an aesthetics of the everyday produced by things that, rather than being isolated from other things and made the focus of concentrated attention, remain in the background. Such things give us "pleasure through a kind of comforting stability, through the feeling of being at home and taking pleasure in carrying out normal routines in a setting that is 'safe'" (2005, 50). According to Haapala, these familiar surround-ings allow us to feel "homey and in control." Although this feeling can seem trivial ("there's no place like home," after all), Haapala points out that it has a surprising degree of importance for us, and he explains this in virtue of a deep existential connection between our sense of self and the everyday environment with which we interact.

Haapala's "aesthetic of the everyday" was not proposed with Design specifically in mind, but it does seem relevant given the everydayness of much Design. Does it provide us with a useful conception of the aesthetics of Design? In one sense, the kind of comforting familiarity that Haapala points out does seem to be a factor in much contemporary Design. As an example, consider the prevalence of skeumorphism, which is the inclusion of Design fea-tures that are not functionally relevant, but which *were* functionally relevant in an earlier version of the object. Consider, for example, smartphone calculator apps that appear to have physical buttons, as pocket calculators did, or push-button phones that maintain the physical form of older, rotary dial telephones. Such Design clearly aims to create a feeling of comfort and familiarity, if not nostalgia, in the user.

However, there is clearly more to the aesthetics of Design than such qualities: Design objects can be elegant, dynamic, striking, bold and so forth. A deeper problem with Haapala's account is that the comforting familiarity of which he speaks appears rather too easy to achieve. For on this view, it seems that virtually anything that has been around long enough will eventually become aesthetically pleasing, once we get accustomed to it. Indeed, Haapala notes that an Alvar Aalto building in his native Helsinki, which he initially found ugly, eventually just ceased to bother him aesthetically. And there is yet a further concern with Haapala's view, which is whether the kind of pleasure he describes is really *aesthetic* at all. Many things give us pleasure – food, drink, sex, sleep, success – yet we do not generally classify these as aesthetic.

This same sort of worry arises for other recent attempts to rethink the concept of the aesthetic. Yuriko Saito, for example, documents the difficulty of applying traditional aesthetic theories to everyday Design items. As a result, she takes a much broader conception of the aesthetic. She writes, "In the realm of the aesthetic, I am including any reactions we form toward the sensuous and/or design qualities of any object, phenomenon, or activity" (2007, 9). However, this conception is so broad that it threatens to trivialize the notion altogether: throwing up after smelling a foul substance, or getting angry upon seeing a spelling mistake, would apparently qualify as aesthetic responses (see also Forsey 2013, 224).

At this point, it seems that the aesthetics of Design is caught in a paradox: if we are to explicate the concept of the aesthetic in a satisfactory way, we must appeal to some sort of *extraordinary* experience, as do the theories given by Stolnitz and Beardsley. But if we do that, then most Design will fail to have aesthetic value, given that we characteristically engage with it in ordinary, rather than extraordinary, situations (Parsons 2012).

There is one more conception of the aesthetic, however, which may offer a way out of this philosophical dead-end. This is the position sometimes referred to as "aesthetic realism" (Levinson 1984, 1994, 2001; for a general overview of the view, see Schellekens 2012). On this view, there exist aesthetic properties, which are, as Jerrold Levinson describes them, "certain looks or feels or impressions or appearances that emerge out of lower-order perceptual properties" (2001, 61). By "lower-order perceptual properties" here, Levinson means properties such as color and shape: the idea is that an aesthetic property like gracefulness is a "real" property that "emerges from" these more ordinary perceptual qualities.

Levinson explains this key notion of emergence in the following way: "aesthetic attributes are ontologically distinct from whatever structural bases support them, and . . . they emerge from them without in any sense including or comprising them in what they are" (1984, 97). There are two parts to this idea. The first is simply that an aesthetic quality, the gracefulness of a line say, is a distinct quality from other qualities the line might have: being curved, being thin, and so on.[6] So the fact that a line is thin and curved does not entail that it is therefore graceful. The second idea is that, although aesthetic properties are distinct from other non-aesthetic properties, they are nonetheless "supported by" those properties. Thus, a line is graceful, if it is, in virtue of having properties like being curved and being thin.

Ontological niceties aside, the important thing about these aesthetic properties, for our purposes, is that they are "objective," in the sense that they are more aptly described as properties of the things we perceive, rather than merely subjective responses to those objects, such as approvals or evaluations. In a sense, this view is closer to the popular conception of beauty as a mathematical feature of certain objects. However, aesthetic properties are not objective in the sense that mass or shape might be; rather, they are said to be objective in something like the sense that colors are.[7] According to aesthetic realism, there are many such properties, such as elegance, angularity, garishness, dynamism and so on.

The key difference between aesthetic realism and the other views discussed above is that, according to aesthetic realism, some things simply have aesthetic properties, and others do not. No special attitude, response or pleasure is responsible for things having the aesthetic properties they do. Rather, they have those properties in virtue of the way that their "lower-order perceptual properties" are constituted. We simply perceive the aesthetic properties, and perhaps enjoy them, or fail to notice them at all, as we do various other perceptual impressions, such as the colors. This approach fits nicely with Design, where we tend to take in the aesthetics of things in a transient way, as we are busily engaged with our everyday activities.

6.3 Dependent Beauty

Adopting aesthetic realism perhaps resolves the problem, raised in the previous section, of how the practical, functional nature of Design is compatible with aesthetic appreciation. However, a second problem remains, for it is still not clear exactly how function is related to these aesthetic properties that Design objects supposedly possess. The Modernist asserts a robust connection between the two, so that an object's functionality makes it beautiful. But how would the fact that an object has the function of brewing coffee, for example, affect whether or not it was elegant, angular, awkward-looking or plain ugly (Parsons and Carlson 2008, 45–9)?

In thinking about this, some philosophers have taken inspiration from an unlikely source: the ideas of the eighteenth-century philosopher Immanuel Kant. Kant's book *Critique of the Power of Judgment* (1790) was extremely influential on philosophical thinking about the nature of beauty. But at first glance, Kant's theory seems not hospitable at all to an aesthetics of Design, given its use of a particularly strong version of the notion of disinterestedness. On Kant's view, we apparently cannot even have a conception of the object or its purpose when we make what he calls a "pure judgement of taste" concerning its beauty. Rather, the concept of the object must be somehow excluded: as Kant puts it, "the judgement of taste is . . . not a cognitive judgement" ([1790] 2001, 89). However, despite articulating this view early in his book, in section 16 Kant famously qualifies it, distinguishing between what he calls *free* and *dependent* beauty.[8] Whereas free beauty "presupposes no concept of what the object ought to be," dependent beauty "does presuppose such a concept and the perfection of the object in accordance with it" (114). Kant offers several examples of dependent beauty, including the beauty of a human being, the beauty of a horse, and the beauty of certain buildings (Kant mentions churches, palaces and arsenals as examples). For these things, our concept of the object, including its purpose or function, does play a role in our aesthetic judgement of it.

To many, Kant's idea of dependent beauty seems to provide just the kind of connection between an object's purpose – or function – and its beauty that is required in an aesthetics of Design. However, what exactly Kant intended "dependent beauty" to mean is a vexed issue amongst scholars. Several differing interpretations of Kant's account of dependent beauty have been offered, each involving a different relation between form and purpose. One prominent interpretation, offered by Paul Guyer, holds that purpose, or function, serves to constrain what it is that we can find beautiful in an object (Guyer 1979, 247; 2002a; 2002b). On this view, if a certain form is incompatible with the object's function, then we cannot find it beautiful, even if, in other contexts, we would find that same form appealing. In support of this interpretation, Guyer points to passages such as this: "One would be able to add much to a building that would be pleasing in the intuition of it," Kant writes, "if only it were not supposed to be a church" ([1790] 2001, 115).

This account gives us a relation between beauty and function, but perhaps not quite the sort of relation that the Modernist would like. For the Modernist notion is that an object's functionality is what, in some way, makes it beautiful. But on Guyer's interpretation of dependent beauty, the function of the object is not involved in making the object beautiful (if it is beautiful); rather, it is merely a "negative" constraint that rules out certain forms from being beautiful. Whatever beauty Design objects would possess, on this account, would remain a free beauty, wholly detached from the object's function or purpose. Designers could "ornament" their creations using colors or shapes that are pleasing, as long as they are not inappropriate with respect to the object's function. Another way to put the point is that, on this view, function can only get in the way of beauty.[9]

A different interpretation of dependent beauty, perhaps more amenable to the Modernist, is given by Robert Wicks (1997). To contrast it with Guyer's account, Wicks describes his interpretation as an "internal" one, according to which a thing's function plays some sort of role in its being beautiful. A key idea in his interpretation is the *contingency* of an object's form in relation to its purpose. "The defined purpose of the object is an abstract concept," Wicks writes, "and as such can therefore never fully determine every contingent detail of its concrete instantiation" (393). So if an object's purpose, or its function, is to allow a person to sit down, this purpose or function is never able to fully specify what the form of the object must be. This contingency of form leads to an experience of beauty, Wicks suggests, when "we compare the given form to other contingent forms . . . which we bring forth in our imagination" (392). This "running through of possible images of the object" (393) results in beauty when "we appreciate . . . the contingency of the way the object realizes its purpose" (393). As an example, Wicks cites how we "appreciate how a mathematical theorem is simple and elegant only with respect to other possible ways to complete the proof" (392). This account makes beauty truly dependent upon function in the sense that it arises from a consideration of the function itself, in relation to the form (and, in particular, to the form's contingency in relation to the function).

Wicks's conception of dependent beauty has its attractions – Jane Forsey (2013) in particular has made Wicks's interpretation central in her account of the aesthetics of Design. But Wicks's account has a special appeal for the Modernist. As mentioned, Wicks's account turns on the idea that the form of any object is contingent: its function could have been realized in a wide variety of different forms. This is nothing other than the notion of the underdetermination of form by function, which we found, earlier on in this chapter, causing trouble for the Modernist. In a curious reversal of fortune, Wicks's account turns this problem into an advantage for the Modernist view. For now, the very fact that the form of Design objects *cannot* "follow" function turns out to be what makes them beautiful!

However, Wicks's conception of dependent beauty faces some serious problems. One is that the "imaginative run through" of the possible forms that could realize a given function, which figures so prominently in his account, simply does not seem to be part of what happens when we experience aesthetic value in Design (Guyer 1999). When we experience a bowl, a car or a household appliance as beautiful, it doesn't seem that we have a "mental slideshow" of alternative forms playing in our heads.[10]

We might just drop this element of Wicks's view, and hold that, for us to experience dependent beauty, we need not *imagine* alternative forms for the object. Rather, it could be sufficient for us to know (or believe) that there are other forms. Forsey, in making use of Wicks's view, gestures in this direction when she says that "to make a considered judgement of the thing we must *know* or at least imagine other contingent ways its function could have been realized and judge it against a backdrop of past attempts" (2013, 184–5; my emphasis). However, even with this qualification in place, another problem arises regarding the source of the aesthetic value on Wicks's account. If it is true, as Wicks claims, that form is always contingent with regard to function, then it would seem that every Design object would automatically be beautiful. But it is hard to see how the mere fact that an object could have had some different form would suffice to give it any aesthetic value.

Wicks himself, in fact, appeals to something beyond the mere contingency of form as a source of aesthetic value. In his example of the mathematical proof, he says that we "appreciate how a mathematical theorem is simple and elegant only with respect to other possible ways to complete the proof" (1997, 392). This places the weight squarely on notions such as simplicity and elegance: something has dependent beauty not merely because, given its function, it could have had a different form; rather, it is dependently beautiful because, given its function, it has a particularly *simple* or *elegant* form.

This has some plausibility: we have certain expectations as to how a particular function could be realized, and when an object's form defeats them, by being strikingly minimalist or cleverly economical, it appears unexpectedly elegant or simple, and hence aesthetically appealing. With this move, however, the notion of dependent beauty sheds its Kantian skin, and is revealed to be something quite familiar: the idea that Design objects are aesthetically attractive when their form is as simple as it can be, given their function.

One worry about this view concerns the concept of simplicity, which, notoriously, turns out to be not so simple upon philosophical reflection. When we speak of a form that is simple in relation to its function, how should this be understood? Should this be taken to mean a form that has a minimal number of components, or a form that allows operation with a minimal number of steps? These two forms of simplicity, in some cases, pull in different directions. Also, merely counting the number of components seems insufficient as a measure of simplicity: consider two identical lamps, having the same Design except that one has a base that is 150 percent larger than the other. Surely we want to say that the one with the smaller base is a simpler Design, insofar as it spares material that the other deploys to no use.

Such worries about how to characterize the notion of simplicity could perhaps be answered by again appealing to aesthetic realism. If elegance and simplicity are aesthetic properties, and such properties are emergent, in the sense described above, then perhaps it is misguided to worry about specifying exactly which non-aesthetic properties characterize them. For it will be generally true that aesthetic properties, given their emergent nature, cannot be characterized in this way.

Setting such worries to one side, we can ask how this conception of the aesthetics of Design fits with the Modernist hope that beauty will emerge effortlessly, as a by-product of the pursuit of functional Design. The thing to notice here is that it is not the functionality of an item that renders it beautiful: rather, it is the item's economy, or frugality with respect to its form. As far as functionality goes, for most cases of Design more and less complex designs will be equally viable. So once again the Modernist's hope remains elusive.

In any case, we have reason to continue scrutinizing the relation between function and aesthetic value. For, even granting the kind of elegance or simplicity discussed by Wicks and Forsey, we must wonder whether we can't say more about this connection. Is this simplicity or elegance all there is to the aesthetics of Design? Dependent beauty, interpreted in this way, gives us an ideal for Design aesthetics according to which objects are as simple as possible. But this is a rather narrow ideal, and a recipe for a rather homogeneous world of Design objects. Surely, one might think, there is more to the aesthetics of Design than this.

6.4 Functional Beauty

For those unsatisfied with the aesthetic austerity of the dependent beauty account described in the previous section, some broader conception of the aesthetics of Design must be found. Some recent efforts in this direction have centered on the concept of "functional beauty." Parsons and Carlson (2008), for example, develop this notion in a way that allows us to generalize on the case of elegance described by Wicks. As mentioned, in that case, we understand how function alters the appearance of the object in terms of its form relating to, and defeating, certain expectations we have about objects with that function – or, as we might alternatively say, objects belonging to the same "functional category."

Adopting some concepts and terminology from Kendall Walton (1970), Parsons and Carlson say that, for a given type of functional object, we can specify certain features that are *standard* for that type, some that are *contra-standard*, or highly unexpected, and some that are *variable*. A feature is standard for a category just in case its absence tends to disqualify the item from the category, contra-standard if its presence tends to so disqualify it, and variable just in case its presence or absence is irrelevant to category membership. So, for example, given that we see an object as belonging to the functional category of "chair," its having legs would be a standard feature of it, being covered in spikes would be contra-standard, and being red would be variable. These differing labels for the properties we perceive in objects reflect differing expectations about their presence in that sort of object.[11] These expectations give us a way to connect our aesthetic experience of objects with our understanding of their function: the aesthetic properties we perceive the object to have will, in some cases, be a matter not only of the non-aesthetic properties we perceive in the object (having legs, being red and so on), but also of whether we perceive those properties as standard, contra-standard or variable.

A number of complications and caveats arise here. For one thing, we need to acknowledge that we can view things as belonging to multiple categories at once. Thus, in the case of art, we may see a particular painting in the general category of "painting" as well as in more specific ones such as "Cubist work" or "portrait." The aesthetic properties of the object will be a function of the total categorization of the work. Also, the ways in which aesthetic properties depend upon this total categorization can be further developed. For example, Walton notes that, although a given may be a variable one, it is possible that "it is nevertheless standard for that category that the variable characteristic falls within a certain range" (1970, 350). In such cases, Walton writes, "the aesthetic effect of the determinate variable property may be colored by the standard limits of the range." In the case of music, for example, piano notes that are sustained, relative to the variable range that we find in piano music, will tend to have a lyrical quality, although, relative to notes made by other instruments, they are very short and unsustained. Finally, it is important to emphasize that this account does not provide rules or sufficient conditions for having an aesthetic property: rather, the claim is merely that objects with these relations to their categories will tend to display these sorts of aesthetic qualities.[12]

We can illustrate this general approach by applying it first to Wicks's example of simplicity and elegance in Design. Imagine a Design object – a coffee pot, say – displaying this sort of aesthetic quality. On Wicks's account, this involves us considering the object's form in light of the various alternative possibilities for realizing its function, and finding it simple in comparison. In our terminology, we could say that the object's non-aesthetic properties (its size, its number of controls and so on) are variable for coffee pots, but at the low end of a variable range.[13] Thus we can encompass Wicks's idea within this framework; we can also, however, use it to identify further ways in which function can affect, or be "translated into," its aesthetic appearance.

A second kind of aesthetic quality that Walton describes in his account is what he describes as "a sense of order, inevitability, stability, correctness" (1970, 348). He sees this quality as tending to occur in works with standard features. In Design, this quality might be seen to occur in architectural works where the various elements seem to occur naturally and inevitably, lending a kind of unity to the work as a whole. Standard features in the object – doorways, hallways, etc. – provide a sense of stability and order in the work. Objects that have a high number of such features, or features that are more standard for the observer (342, n10), tend to possess this quality.[14]

A third kind of functional beauty, according to Parsons and Carlson's account, is the aesthetic quality they call "looking fit." This harkens back to an ancient tradition that viewed things as beautiful when they appeared especially apt for carrying out their function (see Parsons and Carlson 2008, ch. 1). Things have this quality, they claim, when they fail to have perceptual properties that are contra-standard for their functional category, and when they have variable properties that are indicative of a high degree of functionality. Thus, for example, pickup trucks have a particular aesthetic that one can describe in terms of their looking suited to move heavy loads – looking "chunky" and "muscular." The same sort of features would not be aesthetically pleasing in a different sort of vehicle (a hearse, or a sports car, say). It is important to note that the idea of features being "indicative of functionality" is an epistemic one: it refers to the expectation of observers that the features in question are connected to a high degree of function.[15] It may be that the features are not actually so connected, because they don't work at all, or because they are often instantiated in non-functional things, so that they are not reliable indicators of functionality (De Clercq 2013).

A variant of this appealing quality of "looking fit" is a negative quality, which tends to be produced by objects' appearing unsuited to perform their function. When objects are made to look unfit through damage, or shoddy construction, they tend to look aesthetically poorer. This negative quality, however, is closely related to a fourth, more positive variety of functional beauty, which

Parsons and Carlson call "visual tension." This quality arises when things look not quite as they should, insofar as they appear unable to function: some properties of the object appear contra-standard for the functional type, although the object also displays its functionality.[16] As an example, they point to the use of cantilevered design in architecture; or consider forms that seem too simple to realize their function: the "trampoline chair," for example, consists of a single piece of fabric stretched across a frame at a 45° angle to the ground. It simply doesn't look like anything you could sit on, and yet it is a comfortable chair.

The functional beauty approach might also be related to the Modernist's hope for a beauty that flows from functional Design. Could "looking fit" fit this bill? As Parsons and Carlson describe it, this aesthetic quality is not merely a matter of how functional things are, but a matter of how they look. Things will tend to have this quality when they have features that indicate their functionality. So the mere fact that a given Design is functional will not make it beautiful. In the case of the pickup truck, for example, it is the shape of the truck, the size of its tires and so forth, that make it appear powerful. In many cases, however, features that make an object function will also make it appear functional, as when making a chair more comfortable by adding padding to it makes it look more comfortable, or adding supports to a bridge to make it sturdier also makes it look sturdier. On this view, the pursuit of functionality will not always produce this sort of beauty, but there are instances in which it will.

The functional beauty account does emphasize the variety of ways function can affect our perception of the object's form, and hence its aesthetic value. What is distinctive about the aesthetics of Design, on this view, is not merely a quest for simplicity or elegance: rather, Design involves a multiplicity of ways in which form and function can relate to each other.

6.5   Good Taste in Design

Our discussion of aesthetics in Design so far has focused on philosophical issues surrounding the nature of the aesthetic and its relation to function. However, some may feel that this has missed the really crucial issue: whether we can truly say that some Design works are aesthetically better than others. If we grant that we can make aesthetic judgements about Design items, based in part on their functional nature, do we want to say that some people are able to make such judgements more correctly than others, or should we regard all opinions on aesthetic matters as equally valid? A traditional, and useful, way to frame this issue is in terms of the notion of Taste – the capacity for making judgements about aesthetic qualities (Korsmeyer 2013). Are all Tastes equally valid, or do some have better Taste than others, being more able to "get it right" about the aesthetic value of Design objects? Still another way to put the same question is to ask whether there are *facts* about whether a given Design is aesthetically good, or not.

This issue is by no means particular to Design objects, of course: it applies to aesthetic judgement in general. Historically, most discussion of the issue has centered on the aesthetic appreciation of works of art and the view that some people, perhaps people with relevant expertise and sensitivity (capable art critics, for example), have better Taste in art than the average person: they are more likely to determine the truth concerning the aesthetic value of a particular work of art than the average person would be. The same issue, however, arises all the time with respect to the aesthetic value of Design objects, as well as art. In particular, it often arises in the interaction between Designer and client, given the particular nature of Design activity. The client may have a particular Taste that he or she would like to see satisfied, whereas the Designer may have a quite different idea as to what would be aesthetically appropriate. Furthermore, the Designer's view is apt to be grounded in his or her experience and expertise. This produces a very familiar tension between Designer and client.

The problem of Taste is a very large issue in aesthetics, and connects to issues about normativity and value that are fundamental to philosophy as a whole. Therefore, I cannot do justice to it here; rather I will simply provide an overview of the two main positions and identify some of the principal arguments offered for each, relating them to the particular domain of Design.

On one side of the debate, we have the view that all Tastes are equally valid: no aesthetic judgement concerning a Design item can be said to be any more "correct" or "true" than any other. In support of this view, it can be pointed out that there is a conspicuous amount of disagreement in matters of Taste: whereas some praise a particular Design – the Juicy Salif, for example – as aesthetically outstanding, others think it aesthetically worthless. This, it could be said, suggests that in discussions of Taste we are not in the realm of fact, since where there are facts we should expect some consensus of opinion to form. Indeed, proponents of this view typically claim that judgements of aesthetic value are subjective rather than objective. One way to articulate this is to say that, although they appear to be judgements about the *object* (the Juicy Salif), they are actually judgements about the feelings, attitudes or pleasures of the *subject* (the person making the judgement). On this view, when someone says, "The juicy salif is beautiful," they are really talking about themselves, and the particular likes and dislikes that they have, rather than the Juicy Salif.[17]

This view, that aesthetic judgements are subjective rather than objective, entails that judgements of aesthetic value are not open to rational dispute. If, when I say "The juicy salif is beautiful," I am really saying something like "I really like the juicy salif," then no one else can challenge my claim. For who could be a better judge of what I prefer than I am? As the American philosopher Curt Ducasse put it, "Judgements of beauty . . . have to do with the relation of the object judged to the individual's own pleasure experience, of which he himself is the sole possible observer and judge" (1966, 286). On this view, any attempt to privilege one person's aesthetic judgement over another's can only involve an appeal to non-aesthetic factors. For instance, we might say that this person's Taste is better than another's because he or she has a higher social status, which we esteem, or because we admire that person for some other reason. Although such statements may seem, on the surface, to be about aesthetic value, in reality this is an illusion.

The other position in this debate is the view that all Tastes are not equal. A classic, and currently very influential, statement of this view is the essay "Of the standard of taste" (1757) by the Scottish philosopher David Hume. In his discussion, Hume notes both the existence of widespread disagreement concerning matters of Taste, and the idea that Taste is subjective, concerning feeling or, as he puts it, "sentiment." "Beauty is no quality in things themselves," Hume writes; "It exists merely in the mind which contemplates them; and each mind perceives a different beauty" ([1757] 2006, 347). Despite these factors, however, Hume ultimately rejects the view that all Tastes are equal. His reason is that, in certain cases, it is simply agreed that certain judgements of Taste are true and correct. One of his examples is the judgement that the poetry of John Milton is better than that of the now obscure poet Ogilby. A more contemporary example along similar lines would be the judgement that a drug-store romance novel is inferior to Shakespeare's *Hamlet*. The truth of such claims, Hume notes, is no more open to reasonable dispute than plainly "factual" claims such as "A mountain is taller than a molehill." When we consider such examples, Hume suggests, "The principle of the natural equality of tastes is then totally forgot, and while we admit it on some occasions, where the objects seem near an equality, it appears an extravagant paradox, or rather a palpable absurdity, where objects so disproportioned are compared together" (348).

We can reinforce Hume's point by considering more closely those cases where "the objects seem near an equality." If all Tastes were equally valid, then, to the extent that people are reasonable, there should be no critical disputes about aesthetic merit in such cases. But, even being generous about the existence of unreasonable people, such dispute is everywhere: people argue vigorously about whether one book or film is superior to another. Furthermore, when people dispute about the aesthetic value of things, they offer reasons for their judgements, reasons that point out salient features of *the object* in question, in hopes of getting the other party to see the aesthetic value that is, apparently, there in *the object*. On the view that all Tastes are equally valid, none of this should occur, and yet it undeniably does.[18]

Such considerations, in Hume's estimation, are reason enough to reject the view that all Tastes are equally valid. However, it leaves him needing to give some account of what good Taste is, who possesses it and how we might go about cultivating it. As Hume puts it, "It is natural for us to seek a Standard of Taste; a rule, by which the various sentiments of men may be reconciled; at least, a decision afforded, confirming one sentiment, and condemning another" (347). Hume's general view on knowledge leads him to turn to empirical observation, rather than a priori speculation, as the source of our knowledge of this standard. In particular, Hume claims that we can come to know the Standard of Taste by observing the judgements of a particular group of people that he refers to as "ideal critics" or "true judges" of beauty.

Hume describes the "true judges" in terms of five characteristics. They possess "delicacy of imagination," the capacity to notice subtle or "minute qualities" in the object. They have had their judgement "improved by practice," and "perfected by comparison": they have experience evaluating works of art, and in drawing comparisons between a wide variety of works. True judges are also possessed of "strong sense," or a general reasonableness and intelligence, that allows them to understand the work they are appreciating. Finally, the true judge is free from any prejudice, such as hostility toward the work's political stance or personal animus against the author, that would thwart her attempt to provide a true assessment of its merits. People with these qualities provide us, Hume claims, with our best guide in matters of Taste: "Strong sense, united to delicate sentiment, improved by practice, perfected by comparison, and cleared of all prejudice, can alone entitle critics to this valuable character; and the joint verdict of such, wherever they are to be found, is the true standard of taste and beauty" (355). This passage is a little misleading, since on the standard interpretation of his views, the joint verdict of the true judges doesn't *constitute* the standard of taste; rather, the standard consists in "general principles of taste." These principles, which we can, in theory, come to know through empirical experience, identify certain things that are "naturally calculated to give pleasure" ([1757] 2006, 350). Ultimately, then, what is truly beautiful, for Hume, is that which is suited to please everyone.

How do we square these two conceptions of the standard of Taste – that which pleases everyone, and that which pleases the true judges? Hume's idea is that, although the beautiful is suited to please everyone, only the true judges are in the right state to experience this pleasure. He appeals to the analogy of color to explain:

> If, in the sound state of the organ, there be an entire or a considerable uniformity of sentiment among men, we may thence derive an idea of the perfect beauty; in like manner as the appearance of objects in day-light, to the eye of a man in health, is denominated their true and real colour, even while colour is allowed to be merely a phantasm of the senses. (350)

Although colors do not exist in the physical world, but only as sensations in the mind, or as a "phantasm of the senses" as Hume puts it, we nonetheless talk of things having "true and real" colors, and of making errors in judging color. Certain objects are naturally fitted to produce the sensation of a particular color in the human mind when perceived: this is their true or real color. Most of us are usually in the right conditions to perceive these true and real colors of things, but when we are not (in bad lighting, or certain kinds of ill health), our judgements of color can be wrong. The case of beauty is parallel: certain things (beautiful things) are naturally fitted to give pleasure to the human mind when perceived. But, in contrast to the case of color, most of us are generally *not* in the right condition to perceive beauty: our lack of experience, delicacy of imagination and our prejudice interfere with the operation of the "general principles of taste," and cause our judgements to err. Only the true judges are free from these impediments, and thus it is to them that we must turn for insight into what is truly beautiful.[19]

6.6 Bad Taste

Even if we grant Hume's argument for the existence of good Taste, however, there is a further philosophical issue to consider. We might admit that the true judges like what is truly beautiful, and that those of us who like different things like something that is not truly beautiful, but which we mistakenly perceive to be beautiful. But we might yet ask why the rest of us should *care* about this mistake. In other words, why should we care about having bad Taste? Say you aren't a true judge. You like things that the true judges don't like. You have bad taste. Should this bother you? In response to this, the defender of good Taste might point out that you miss the beauty of beautiful works. However, you might reply that you still get pleasure from what you like, even though it isn't really beautiful. So, you might ask, what is the incentive for you to change?[20]

In fact, one could make a strong case that you would be *better off* to have bad Taste. We can see this by noting two points from the American philosopher Curt Ducasse. The first is the idea that, although becoming a true judge gives one the ability to discern, and enjoy, true beauties, becoming a true judge also robs one of something. Ducasse, who calls true judges "connoisseurs," writes: "Connoisseurship makes possible aesthetic pleasures. . . . which persons who are not connoisseurs cannot experience. But it also makes impossible the aesthetic pleasures which none but the aesthetically less sensitive souls can taste" (1966, 282). So, by becoming a true judge, you come to see the beauty in Shakespeare's plays, but you lose the pleasure you used to get from romance novels before you became a true judge. Appreciating the features of good novels makes you more sensitive to the features of bad ones: the flaws that pass by the unschooled give pain to the expert.

A second idea we need to take from Ducasse is the idea that the only way to compare pleasures is in terms of their quantity, or amount. "For a ranking of beauties," Ducasse writes, "there are available only such principles as the relative intensity of the pleasure felt, its relative duration . . . and relative freedom from admixture of pain" (289). Ducasse's point is that pleasures have various causes and effects which we often take into account when comparing them. So we might say that drinking chamomile tea is a better form of pleasure than taking heroin, because the latter has problematic effects (addiction) and morally troublesome origins (the drug trade). But if we consider two pleasures *in themselves*, bracketing their causes and effects, Ducasse says that the only comparison to draw between them, *as pleasures*, is in terms of their degree. Drinking chamomile tea has a different feeling to it than taking heroin, but if we want to compare the two pleasures and rank them, the only way to do that is to appeal to the quantity of pleasure present. Taking heroin is, in that sense, clearly a much greater pleasure than drinking chamomile tea (even if, for other reasons to do with its causes and effects, we desire to resist it). Applying this to the case of good and bad Taste, we can observe that if we compare the pleasure of the true judge and the pleasures of someone with bad Taste, there is no clear reason to think that the latter will be worse off. For people with bad Taste might get a great quantity of pleasure out of the things that they like. Furthermore, there is, it seems, a great deal more aesthetically mediocre and poor stuff from which the person with bad Taste can derive pleasure.

Putting these two points together, we can see that not only is the person with bad Taste not obviously worse off than the true judge, it seems like it might be *better* to have Bad Taste, for the following reason. The true judge is very sensitive, seeing all the flaws in things. But most things aren't very good. So the odds are that he's going to get less pleasure than the rest of us do. Also, becoming a true judge is a lot of work, requiring one to practice, expose oneself to new works, and cultivate the required understanding. So one might think that it's better to forgo the effort: why do all that work for less overall pleasure? Of course, someone might reply that if your taste does not align with that of the true judges, then your aesthetic judgements are liable to be simply wrong. You live, in other words, in a fool's paradise. But this is an empty response. For in this case, it doesn't seem there's anything wrong with living in a fool's paradise (Levinson 2002).

What response could the defender of good Taste give to this skeptical line of thought?[21] One possible response takes issue with the idea that pleasures can only differ in their quantity. Most things, it can be observed, differ in both quantity and quality, and perhaps pleasure should be no exception. This view was famously defended by the nineteenth-century British philosopher John Stuart Mill, who wrote, "It would be absurd that while, in estimating all other things, quality is considered as well as quantity, the estimation of pleasures should be supposed to depend on quantity alone" ([1861] 1979, 8). This is easy enough to say, but how could we possibly assess the *quality* of two pleasures, as opposed to the quantity? Mill famously considered this question with respect to what he called the sensual pleasures (sex, food, sleep, for example) and the higher or intellectual pleasures, those available only to human beings or creatures of equivalent powers (playing chess, doing science, reading novels and so on). To address it, Mill proposed the following test: "If one of two [pleasures] is, by those who are competently acquainted with both, placed so far above the other that they prefer it, even though knowing it to be attended with a greater amount of discontent . . . we are justified in ascribing to the preferred enjoyment a superiority in quality" (8–9). Mill posed his test in terms of the following offer: you can be a happy pig, enjoying as much sensual pleasure as you wish, for the rest of your days, or, you could stay a human being and enjoy a smaller total amount of pleasure that includes some pleasure of the intellectual variety. Mill asserted that no one would choose to become a pig satisfied rather than a human dissatisfied. That is, no one would trade the intellectual pleasures of his life (however imperfect) for any amount of sensual pleasure (i.e., an entire life as a pig). It is important to see that Mill's conclusion from this example is not that intellectual pleasures deliver us a greater quantity of pleasure. For, if we consider only quantity of pleasure, then, at some point, the quantity delivered by the intellectual pleasures of a human life will be outweighed by the vast quantity of sensual pleasure experienced by the pig. Rather, the preference for the intellectual pleasures must be explained by a difference in the quality of the pleasures in question. Thus, Mill says that the intellectual pleasures are *higher* than sensual pleasures.

The defender of good Taste might attempt to apply Mill's test to aesthetic matters, in the following way. We want to compare the quality of pleasures attained from enjoying that which is truly beautiful (that liked by the true judges) with the pleasures attained from enjoying that which is not truly beautiful. To do this, we find those who have experienced both pleasures: the true judges. And we must then ask them: would you give up the pleasure you get from enjoying great works for a lifetime packed with enjoying mediocre ones? This is an empirical question. But it is not implausible to speculate that few if any true judges would accept such a deal, even if it meant getting less pleasure overall, just as most people would reject Mill's offer to become a "pig satisfied." So, we might conclude that the pleasure of true beauty is, indeed, a pleasure higher in quality. And, if this is the case, then perhaps "getting it right" is worth the effort after all.

7

Ethics

So far, we have investigated some key aspects of Design, attempting along the way to assess the various philosophical claims about Design implicit in Modernist thinking. Although we have covered aesthetics, expression and function, there is one very broad area about which we haven't yet said much: ethics. In this chapter, we will take up this important topic, but, before we do, a bit of terminological clarification is in order.

In its everyday use, the term "ethics," and its sister word "morality," perhaps suggest a set of more or less explicit rules or norms which constrain our public behavior. To behave in an ethical manner is, in this sense, to follow the relevant rules of conduct. In philosophical contexts, however, the term is used a broader way to refer to a concern with the question of how one should live, or what a good human life consists in. This broader sense of the term incorporates the narrower sense, since rules or norms that constrain how we should treat others are one important aspect of the way we live. But it also includes much more, and relates to questions about what sort of person we should strive to be, which activities are worthwhile and which are not, and so on.

Design is relevant to ethics in both senses, but particularly in the broader sense, given that it has a great effect upon how we live through its creation of our material, and, increasingly, our immaterial or virtual, environment. As we have seen, this "mediation" of our experience through technology occurs not only when Design makes a new kind of deliberate action possible, but also through the more subtle ways that Designs shape our unreflective behavior and thinking (Verbeek 2005).

There are a number of ways to explore the connections between Design and ethics; in this chapter, I focus on three.[1] The first concerns perhaps the most obvious point of connection: the way that Designers confront and handle ethical rules, regulations and norms that apply to the objects they are creating. The second involves something more fundamental: the Designer's very choice of what to create. This second issue takes us into a philosophical investigation of consumerism and the difference between needs and wants. The third issue again takes us into a deep philosophical issue: whether a consideration of the role of Design in how we live implies a fundamental reconsideration of the very concept of ethics itself. In the course of our discussion, we will also examine the Modernist's claim (or hope) that the pursuit of functional Design will, in some way, lead us to ethically better Design.

7.1   Applied Ethics and Design

It is beyond dispute that to create certain kinds of products, or to Design them in certain ways, would be unethical. To Design an explosive device in bright colors that would appeal to children, for example, would very clearly be wrong. Such cases of inherently unethical Design are, thankfully, as rare as they are extreme.[2] More common are cases where the ethical problem is not with the object *per se*, but in the fact that Designers have negligently compromised user safety in some way, usually as a way of cost-cutting. Also familiar are those cases where an ethical problem is connected with some particular way of using (or misusing) the object: handguns would be an obvious example. One can argue that it is not the production, or use, of the object *per se* that threatens ethical norms, but only certain *mis*uses of the object. Hence the infamous slogan of the National Rifle Association, that "Guns don't kill people, people kill people." On the other hand, some insist that the problem is not merely one of misuse and that the very production and "standard use" of handguns (as concealed deterrents, for example) is itself unethical.

These sorts of discussions clearly carry Designers into the territory of ethics. Before we explore this terrain further, however, it will be useful to distinguish three traditional sub-divisions of the field: meta-ethics, normative ethics and applied ethics. *Meta-ethics* is the branch of philosophy that attempts to understand, in a very general way, the nature of ethics itself. Questions in this field include: What is a moral norm? and What is the basis for moral judgement? (Miller 2003). *Normative ethics*, while not attempting to address these very fundamental questions, attempts to spell out the most general principles or frameworks for ethical decision-making. One such principle, widely debated in normative ethics, is the Utilitarian principle that actions are morally right when they contribute to human happiness (Mill [1861] 1979). Finally, *applied* or *practical ethics* seeks to understand particular moral problems and determine whether particular actions (abortion, or euthanasia, for example) are morally permissible or not. Overlap between ethics and Design typically falls in the last category: the ethical issue around producing handguns, for example, is not a meta-ethical one, nor an issue of normative ethics, concerning a general moral principle or framework, but an issue of the ethical status of a particular action – producing handguns.

This sort of issue typically arises when a new type of thing allows a new sort of action that runs up against socially sanctioned ethical norms. As the things Designers create, and the actions that those things make possible, are subject to society's ethical norms and rules, this means that Design has an important ethical aspect. However, this ethical dimension of Designing is sometimes obscured, in the popular consciousness at least, by the influence of a particular way of thinking about technology and its development – the idea of technological determinism. Technological determinism is the idea that the development of technology is not controlled by human thought and decision-making: rather, it is the other way around. The development of technology has a "life of its own," and once technologies are in place they shape the nature of society and its decisions. On this view, although humans may debate about the merits of new technologies, and whether they should be pursued, this is ultimately beside the point, as whatever can be made, given current scientific and technical knowledge, eventually will be made.[3]

However, even if some version of technological determinism is true, this would not entail that ethical deliberation about technology is pointless. Even if technology is in some part driven by "internal forces," social values and decisions undoubtedly play a role as well. Feng offers the example of the development of microprocessors, which supposedly follow "Moore's Law" of doubling in power every 18 to 24 months. This development seems to be constrained only by internal factors to do with technical improvements in processing speeds. Yet, Feng observes, the development would not occur were it not for heavy investment in processing research. Thus, social values and demands also play a crucial, if not always highly visible, role (Feng 2000; Neeley and Luegenbiehl 2008). Furthermore, even if there were a kind of inevitability about what things will be produced in the future, there are still many ethically important choices to be made about *how* those things will be Designed. Van Gorp and van de Poel (2008, 79–80) offer the simple example of Designing a photocopier. Does one make the default setting "one-sided printing" or "two-sided printing?" While the choice may seem trivial, it could have enormous implications for paper use and thereby for environmental sustainability.

A second factor serving to obscure the ethical aspect of Designing is the fact that, although cases of items with some dangerous use (or misuse), such as handguns, attract much attention, the bulk of the applied ethics of Design concerns more mundane matters of safety: it is unethical to Design a device that is unsafe and puts people at an unacceptable risk. But this ethical area might seem an unproblematic one from the philosophical point of view, given the existence of legal product standards for many types of goods. The Designer may merely consult the relevant product codes and ensure that his or her Design is safe, without any need for ethical deliberation.

However, the nature of Design as a creative activity means that, in some cases at least, things will not be so straightforward, since there simply will not be extant codes and regulations covering the new object (Van Gorp and van de Poel 2008). A narrow focus on safety standards also obscures a major complicating factor in the applied ethics of Design, which is that safety is far from the only relevant ethical value. Others include freedom, availability, consumer choice, privacy and environmental sustainability (as in the above example of the copier button). The applied ethics of Design can involve all of these values, given that Design has the potential to affect our ability to realize them.

Nor is applied Design ethics simply a matter of satisfying whatever ethical norms society has instituted, or whatever ethical values it happens to hold. For these different ethical norms and values can, and often do, conflict with one another as well as with functional criteria for Design. For example, from the point of view of functionality, it seems that Designers should always strive for the highest-quality goods possible. But as Bakker and Loui (1997) argue, this might not always result in realizing certain ethical values: a Design might fulfill its function very effectively, for example, but do so inefficiently, consuming a great deal of resources and therefore compromising environmental sustainability. Also, inefficiency might make the item more expensive, reducing consumer choice. The operation of a perfectly functional Design might also, through its normal operation, compromise user freedom, in the way that seatbelt-linked ignition systems do. Security systems that are very effective in detecting potential threats to public safety can compromise privacy, and so on (on value conflicts in engineering design, see van de Poel 2009). A very large part of the ethics of Design consists in trying to clarify and resolve these conflicts between different values, in order to determine whether the use of a new item would be appropriate, or not.

7.2 Consumerism, Needs and Wants

This last point in our discussion of applied ethics in Design has an important implication for the Modernist's claim that purely functional Design will be ethically good Design. Clearly this thesis cannot be maintained, if we consider the ethical values relevant to Design in the broadest sense. As mentioned, highly functional Designs can negatively affect freedom, privacy and other ethical values. However, perhaps the Modernist claim could be understood in a more modest sense, as the claim that purely functional Design would be ethically beneficent *in one respect*, by combating wasteful consumerism.

The thought here would be that if we eschew the expressionist and aesthetic employments of Design, and instead pursue purely functional Design, a great wasting of resources will be avoided. There is clearly some truth in this, since much consumption is generated by the use of consumer goods as expressive or aesthetic aids. A classic example is the automobile, still redesigned year after year in the hopes of convincing people to replace their existing vehicles. However, this version of the Modernist's claim is too modest, for a Design practice that dispensed with aesthetic and expressive aims could still be massively wasteful of resources by producing functionally excellent designs for pointless devices. Consider, for example, the leaf blower. A well-designed leaf blower might be very effective at carrying out its function: blowing leaves around. The problem with devices like this one is not that they are created for aesthetic or expressive reasons, but that the functions they fulfill are, in some sense, gratuitous or unnecessary.[4] There is no need to blow leaves around, given that one can rake them into a pile.

Thus, if Modernism is to vindicate even the more modest version of its claim, it must distinguish between those functions that are valid and those that are unnecessary: the most obvious way to do this would be to appeal to the conceptual distinction between *wants* and *needs*. The Modernist could then claim that functional Design that addresses needs leads to ethically good Design, at least in the sense of reducing consumption. In a sense this distinction is already present in the Modernist view, for the very rejection of expression is tantamount to the view that expression through Design, while certainly something that many people want, is not something that they actually need.

The very distinction between want and need, however, is contested. Indeed, it can be hard to see this distinction sometimes in everyday language, where the terms "want" and "need" are often used rather loosely and interchangeably. Writers on Design, for instance, will sometimes tackle the question "Do you need new Design item X?" when really the issue they are addressing is: "Given its novel features, will you want Design item X badly enough to pay what it costs?" This casual use of the term "need" aside, however, there does appear to be a distinction, in our linguistic practices, between the concepts of want and need (Wiggins and Derman 1987). This distinction shows itself in several ways, firstly in the fact that we often acknowledge that people want things that they don't need (a third pair of red running shoes) and that, conversely, people need things that they don't want (education or a medical treatment, for instance).

A second aspect of the distinction between needs and wants, which helps to explain the first, is that the former are taken to be more objective than the latter. For someone to *want* something is merely for *that person* to be a certain way: it is for him to have a certain psychological relation to that thing. For someone to *need* something, more is required than that the subject have a certain psychological relation to it; the thing in question must be in some way "called for" by real features of his life situation (Wiggins and Derman 1987, 62). This is not to say that desires cannot also be called for by features of our life situation, for we often want things we need (food, sleep and so on). But wants needn't possess this objective aspect, whereas needs must.

This second difference leads naturally toward a third, which is that needs have a kind of priority over wants. As one philosopher puts it, "an assertion that something is needed tends to create an impression of an altogether different quality, and to have a substantially greater moral impact, than an assertion that something is desired" (Frankfurt 1984, 1). Thus, if one person desires a new espresso machine, and another desires sufficient food to keep himself alive, we naturally give precedence to satisfying the second person, since he needs the thing in question, whereas the first person does not need a new espresso machine, but merely wants one. This is so even if the psychological relation of desire that each has toward the object is the same (even if the man who wants the espresso machine wants it more intensely than the other man wants food to stay alive, perhaps because of pain and despair, he still has nothing like an equal claim to it). This idea is sometimes referred to as the "Principle of Preference" (Frankfurt 1984, 3).

Given that we can draw the distinction between wants and needs, however, the question arises as to what things fall into the latter category. In philosophical discussions, attention is often focused on the so-called "basic needs" of food, air, water and shelter. Everyone would agree that these are bona fide needs of human beings, and not merely wants, for these things are "called for by objective features of one's life situation" in a very direct way: without them, human beings die. However, "things necessary for survival" is a very narrow conception of need: if mere biological survival is all that is at stake, then humans do not need espresso machines, but neither do they need electricity, or even indoor plumbing. As miserable as forgoing these might make us, we would no doubt survive (as our forebears did).

More to the point, understanding need in terms of the basic needs only is far too narrow a conception of need for use in the Modernist claim, since it would restrict Design to things such as architecture, agriculture and perhaps medicine. While this would no doubt solve the ethical problem of over-consumption, it is too extreme to merit serious consideration.[5] Furthermore, and more importantly, while many Design objects address aims other than the basic needs, they are not thereby unnecessary or gratuitous. For example, neither telephones nor leaf blowers are required for biological survival but, intuitively, the second is a much clearer example of "unnecessary design" than the first. Another way to put the point is that we do use the term "need" to cover more than the basic needs. We therefore require a more widely applicable criterion for being a need, as opposed to a mere want.

One natural strategy here would be to understand a need as something that is not desired merely for its own sake, but is required to achieve some larger end. As Harry Frankfurt puts the idea: "when something is needed it must . . . be possible to specify what it is needed for" (1984, 3). Thus we might say that someone who buys a car in order to get to work and pursue a career is fulfilling a need, but that someone who buys a convertible, "just to have it," is only gratifying a want. In the first case, the object facilitates the realization of a larger goal, whereas in the second case, it does not.

This line of thought is appealing, since it is true that we often broach the question of whether we need something in this fashion, by looking for a larger end to be realized. However, a little reflection shows the futility of this approach, since for almost anything at all one can easily find a "larger aim" for which that thing is essential. Thus the man buying his third convertible can easily rationalize his purchase by saying that it is necessary for him to complete his convertible collection, which it well may be. Generally speaking, it seems that any want can be cast in the form of a need, using this criterion.

The failure of this attempt to find a broader conception of "need" might tempt us to skepticism about the very possibility of doing so. A skeptic might argue as follows: perhaps the concept of "need," if extended any further than the so-called "basic needs," is an empty one. People *want* various things, to a greater or a lesser degree, but nothing that they desire or might desire is really "called for by their life situation" in the objective way that a true (i.e. basic) need is. The skeptic could also add a somewhat cynical explanation for why we insist on using this broader concept of need, in spite of its emptiness. Here the skeptic may say that, aside from the basic needs, the "needs" we speak of are false needs: nothing more than intense desires dressed up in "objective" garb. If this was right, then the concept of need, as it might be deployed in Design, would be an insidious one: when a man says that he needs a new suit, what he really means is just that he really wants one, although he prefers not to come out and simply say this, as doing so would make him feel less justified in acting to satisfy this desire.

7.3 Is Need an Empty Concept?

The skeptical view of needs as no more than intense desires, which was sketched in the previous section, is important to consider. If it is true, then it seems to throw into doubt the thesis that we can reduce consumption by Designing for needs. One problem for this skeptical view has already been noted – the fact that we sometimes want to say that a person needs something even though she doesn't want it at all ("She needs to change her attitude"; "He needs to learn some manners"). These needs, at least, cannot be reduced to desires. However, as we have already seen, wants, like needs, can be construed as necessary for the attainment of some higher end that *is desired*. Thus perhaps the skeptic can say that, in the above cases, a need is something that, given her desires, the person in question *would want*, if she understood her situation rationally.

What then should we make of this skeptical view? The opponent of the skeptic will want to insist that there does seem to be a genuine difference between someone's (false) need for a third convertible and her true need for, say, education, or social skills. The problem is to explain how we can make sense of this apparent difference.

In broaching the distinction between true and false needs, writers on Design and consumerism have sometimes appealed to the *origin* of needs as the crucial factor. Victor Papanek, for instance, writes that "the economic, spiritual, technological, and intellectual needs of a human being are usually more difficult and less profitable to satisfy than the carefully engineered and manipulated 'wants' inculcated by fad and fashion" (1971, 11).[6] Might we not say that false needs are needs that we would fail to recognize, were it not for the influence of some external force, such as advertising? This is an appealing view, given the great power of advertising to instil wants and desires, as well as the number of intuitively false needs associated with advertising. It is easy to think of examples of clever advertising campaigns that lead people to believe that they need the latest product. However, it would be a mistake to understand false needs as those with a particular origin (that is, as those we come to recognize only through some outside influence). A person with a medical condition, or an ignorant person, might never come to recognize that they need medical treatment or education without being influenced by some outside agency. This influence might involve a significant amount of persuasion, just as advertising does. But this would not make their needs any less real.

To distinguish true from false needs, we need to look not to the origin of the associated desire, but to the *value* of that which is desired. An approach of this kind was taken by the ancient Greek philosopher Aristotle, who defines a need as a thing

> without which . . . it is not possible to live, as for instance breathing and nourishment are necessary for an animal, because it is incapable of existing without them: and anything without which it is not possible for good to exist or come to be, or for bad to be discarded or got rid of, as for instance, drinking medicine is necessary so as not to be ill, and sailing to Aegina so as to get money. (1015a20)

In the first part of this quotation, Aristotle gives examples of what we have been calling "basic needs," such as air, food and medical treatment. But the second criteria that he gives for a need – being necessary "for good to exist or come to be" – is general enough to illuminate needs beyond the basic ones.

The core of Aristotle's account is that needs are those things required for us to achieve things of value (things that are good, or worthwhile). Returning to our earlier example, both the person who needs education and the person who needs a third convertible are trying to achieve some higher aim, and both may have been influenced by some external force, but only the former seeks something necessary to achieve something of value. The person who wants the third convertible cannot say that, without it, "good will fail to come to exist," since there is little value or worth in a collection of red convertibles. Of course, such a collection may be *seen by* some as having value (it may even thereby have economic value), and the collector may want such a collection very intensely, and even think that his happiness and fulfillment depend upon it. But this does not make his want into a need, since thinking that something is valuable does not make it so.[7]

If this account of needs provides a response to the skeptical view, however, it also puts a great deal of weight on the Designer's value judgements about the ways in which we should live. If the Designer is to Design, as the Modernist view would hold, only for need, not only has she to sort out ethical values relevant to what she makes, as we discussed in section 7.1 above, but the very decision to make at all implicates her in some kind of conceptualization of the way we ought to live. Thus we are brought back to the lingering idea of the Designer as a sort of seer or philosopher, whose task is not merely to make things or solve problems, but to guide society in some larger way.[8]

The idea that Designers, or anyone for that matter, can pronounce about what counts as "genuine need" invites objections. Colin Campbell, for example, argues that to declare some needs as true and others false is "simply to express a prejudice in favor of one specific conception of the good life," and "will almost certainly lead to the endorsing of traditionalistic, Puritanical and in all probability authoritarian, attitudes" (2010, 283).

Much of this is clearly exaggerated. It is no doubt true that it is easy to be dogmatic about "the good life" or what is worthwhile or valuable, much as it is easy to be dogmatic about other things, such as what is true. But this by no means entails that all claims about value are mere "prejudice": claims about value can be mere prejudice but they can also be well thought out and grounded in good reasons. It is also plainly not true that making judgements of value will lead to authoritarianism: for example, in societies where freedom is valued, judgements about the good will not be foisted upon individuals who may disagree with them, but the fact that such value judgements are not imposed upon everyone does not make them any less judgements of value, or any less correct.[9] However, Campbell's points do have a particular salience in the context of Design, for the Designer, unlike others, gets to embed her determinations of the "good life" in material culture, and, in that sense, imposes them on others.

7.4 Does Design Alter the Moral Landscape?

So far we have seen that ethics can have big implications for Design. We can turn this around and ask whether Design has implications for ethics. Some thinkers have even suggested that taking stock of Design's connection to ethics not only reveals a new area of ethical issues and concerns, but in fact radically changes our understanding of ethics itself. One such view is the idea that the products of Design themselves should be viewed as moral agents.

One of the most important inspirations for this thesis is a famous 1980 essay by Langdon Winner called "Do artifacts have politics?". In that essay, Winner took issue with a widespread view on ethics and technology, which is the view that, although people may use technology in taking certain actions, it is only the actions themselves, and not the artefacts employed, that are properly subject to ethical evaluation. Winner elegantly described the view as follows:

> It is no surprise to learn that technical systems of various kinds are deeply interwoven in the conditions of modern politics . . . But to go beyond this obvious fact and to, at first glance, completely mistaken. We all know that people have politics; things do not. To discover either virtues or evils in aggregates of steel, plastic, transistors, integrated circuits, chemicals and the like seems just plain wrong, a way of mystifying human artifice and of avoiding the true sources, the human sources of freedom and oppression, justice and injustice. (1980, 20)

On this common view, it is conceded that a bit of technology might have political effects. Internet search engines, for example, might be used to gather information on users in a way that corrodes their right to privacy. But, in this case, the common view holds that it would be misleading to say that the technological artefact – the search engine – is unjust. Rather, the injustice is located in a human action – namely, the misuse of that artefact by particular human agents.

Winner acknowledges that this common view seems quite reasonable, but he rejects it on the grounds that it obscures the important role that artefacts play in ethical decision-making. To locate the ethical responsibility only in the decisions of the human agents, Winner argued, misses the fact that certain technologies, in and of themselves, can direct and shape those decisions. Winner offered the example of the highway overpasses built in New York City in the 1950s by Robert Moses. Apparently, these were deliberately built too low for buses to pass underneath, thereby preventing the poorer Black New Yorkers, who did not own cars, from reaching certain areas. In this case, Winner argued, there is a political aspect to the artefact itself. If we focus only on the actions of human agents, on what people in a society do, we fail to account for the ways those actions are shaped, often subtly, by the material environment. For example, if we looked for racism only in the actions of New Yorkers, we would miss the segregation that is quietly being carried out by the overpasses.

In his essay, Winner's concern was mainly with the political aspects of technology, but other authors have extended his general approach to encompass moral as well as political values. The sociologist Bruno Latour, for example, argued that an adequate understanding of morality must include, as well as human agents, non-human agents such as artefacts. "We have been able to delegate to nonhumans . . . values, duties, and ethics," he writes; "It is because of this morality that we, humans, behave so ethically, no matter how weak and wicked we feel we are" (1992, 232). Latour emphasizes the many, often unnoticed, ways in which artefacts "act" in ways that allow us to behave ethically. The speed bump, for example, plays a crucial role in getting drivers to obey the laws and drive safely. Latour insists that, in order to fully understand ethics, we must eliminate the human/non-human distinction and incorporate non-human moral agents into our moral framework. Echoing the views of Winner and Latour, the philosopher Peter-Paul Verbeek maintains, "The conclusion seems justified that artefacts have morality: technologies play an active role in moral action and decision-making" (2008, 93). Verbeek refers to this phenomenon of "the moral agency of technological artefacts" as "material morality."

The notion of material morality demands some close scrutiny, given its great philosophical interest. For it portends nothing less than a conceptual revolution with regard to ethical thinking. Traditionally, philosophers have reserved the title of "moral agent" for a very specific sort of being: creatures capable of rational deliberation and free, intentional choice. As it stands, this means that only human beings count as moral agents (notice also that the requirement of rational deliberation rules out even humans who are children and others incapable of rational deliberation, such as the insane). Further, moral agency, on the traditional view, is intimately linked to moral responsibility. If one acts out of moral agency, then

one is responsible for one's action, and can be subjected to praise
or blame accordingly. However, we do not typically punish artefacts
for "wrongdoing." So it would be a major conceptual shift were we
to do this, as the material morality thesis apparently suggests.

In support of the notion of material morality, it might be pointed
out that our ethical framework has undergone major revolution in
the past. For example, at various times and places, women and slaves
were regarded as unworthy of moral consideration. Furthermore,
and more recently, there has been an expansion in moral concern
to include non-human animals, and even non-sentient parts of the
environment.

However, we should examine these changes carefully. This expansion has not been with respect to what it is to be a moral agent,
subject to responsibilities and worthy of praise or blame. In the case
of expanding moral consideration to non-human animals and non-
sentient entities such as trees or ecosystems, what has been at stake
is not an attribution of moral agency, but rather the quite different
status of *having moral standing*. So although many would argue that
trees or rivers have some moral standing, in that harming them may
be morally wrong, we do not think of bestowing moral praise or
blame on these entities, as we do with moral agents such as adult
human beings. To attribute moral agency to artefacts, then, would
be to significantly alter our conceptual framework in a way that has
no clear precedent.

Given this, we should ask what arguments can be given for, and
against, including artefacts amongst moral agents. Would there be
anything incoherent or problematic about this? One complication
in this debate is its overlap with a central debate in the field of
artificial intelligence, which is whether a computer could possess a
mind, or mental states, in the sense that human beings do. If it is
indeed possible for a computer to possess a mind, in the same sense
that a human does, then it is natural to think that such a computer
would be a moral agent in the same sense that a human being is a
moral agent.[10] However, as Verbeek points out, this debate about
sentient computers is one that we can set aside in a general discussion of material morality (2011, 50). For a sentient computer would
be an artefact of a very specific and sophisticated kind, able to
behave in ways analogous, or even superior, to a human being. But
the question of whether artefacts have moral agency is one raised
about much more mundane artefacts: overpasses, speed bumps and

the like. So the question we need to focus on is whether attributing moral agency to *these artefacts* would be problematic.

One obvious objection to this view is that although such artefacts have effects, they do not really "act," since they cannot form intentions to do anything. Since moral agency requires that the agent perform actions intentionally, or on purpose (having some goal in mind), artefacts of this type cannot be moral agents. In response to this objection, Verbeek notes that the original etymology of the word "intend" is "to direct." He then argues that, since it is clear that artefacts can direct our behavior in various ways (consider the examples of the highway overpass and the speed bump, mentioned above), they can have intentionality.

Against this, one might object that "intentionality," in the context of discussions of moral agency, means much more than merely "directing a course of action." It means directing *one's own* course of action toward some goal or end. As such, it requires a set of psychological states on the part of the agent: beliefs about that course of action and its relation to a goal, as well as some sort of desire that the course of action come about. Without these psychological elements, it might be said, we are simply not discussing "intentional action" in the sense relevant to moral agency. In this sense, it seems that speed bumps and overpasses do not have intentionality, and so cannot be considered moral agents. However, this argument concerning intentions might ultimately be beside the point. After all, one might argue that, whether they have intentions or not, artefacts clearly *do* act in the sense that, when humans act ethically, part of the "work" is done by the artefact (Latour 1992).

A different argument against attributing moral agency to such artefacts is that they lack a crucial attribute of genuine moral agency – freedom. Whereas what artefacts do is determined by causal forces, what humans do is not. Thus Deborah Johnson argues that humans count as moral agents only because of a "mysterious, non-deterministic aspect of moral agency" (2006, 200). Since we have no reason to think that artefacts could ever act in this mysterious non-deterministic way, we have no grounds for attributing moral agency to them. However, this argument is a weak one, relying as it does on the premise that humans possess a "mysterious, non-deterministic agency." Many have argued that the apparent freedom of will that humans possess is an illusion, and that human action is just as determined as what happens to artefacts and physical objects in general. Those who argue this way nonetheless hold that, in some sense, people are moral agents.

Yet another argument against attributing moral agency to artefacts is that moral agency entails moral responsibility, but, as mentioned earlier, it would make no sense to hold artefacts responsible for their "actions." For example, what would it mean to hold something like a speed bump or an overpass responsible? Of course, if such an artefact was doing harm, we would want to eliminate it, and if it were doing some good, we might want to maintain or more widely implement it. But this is not the same as holding it responsible for its actions, as we do with people.

In response to this sort of objection, Floridi and Sanders (2004) argue that the concept of moral agency can be coherently separated from the notion of moral responsibility.[11] In support of this, they point to cases involving dogs and children. We often praise or blame these creatures when they carry out an action that we deem good or bad ("bad dog"), although we recognize that they are not morally responsible for their actions. This seems to show that we have a concept of moral agency – being the source of a morally good or bad action – that does not require moral responsibility. In a similar way, we might say things such as "these speed bumps are good" and "those overpasses are evil," although we do not hold them morally responsible in the way we hold people morally responsible.

This reply to the objection, however, only points to a deeper flaw with the moral agency thesis, even in its more modest formulations. If artefacts are not subject to moral responsibility, then what will be the upshot of turning the focus of our ethical analysis toward them? It must be to make moral responsibility for whatever effects those artefacts have more elusive. A "bad" artefact is one that must be replaced, but who is responsible for this? It is not the artefact, or any other artefact, but must be some human being, a moral agent in the full sense (Johnson 2006; Noorman 2014).

This can be illustrated with regard to Verbeek's example of handguns. Do people kill people, or do guns kill people? Verbeek insists that this traditional question is misguided, for "agency should not be located exclusively in either the gun or the person shooting, but in the assembly of both" (2011, 64). But exactly what is gained by assigning part of the moral agency to the gun? If guns cannot be held responsible, as Verbeek elsewhere seems to admit, then what is to be done about their "bad behavior?" The guns will not respond to our moral reproaches, so some human agent will need to intervene. Who will this be: gun manufacturers? Law-makers? The police? Attributing moral agency to guns does not help address this question but in fact only serves to obscure it. The problem with extending moral agency to artefacts, then, is that it makes it harder for us to focus our ethical analysis where it is *ultimately* needed: on human decisions and actions. Another way to put the point is that it reifies technology into something analogous to human moral agents, when in fact it is not.

But what of the argument, given by Latour, that we must acknowledge the moral agency of artefacts simply because they do so much of our "moral work": that, as Verbeek puts it, "technologies are morally *active*" (2011, 57)? It can certainly be conceded that artefacts do "moral work," in one sense, in that the decisions and actions that people take are certainly affected and shaped by their material environment. However, in another sense, artefacts do no "moral work" at all, for we are not interested in the ways in which artefacts influence human moral behavior in the same way that we are interested in human moral behavior itself. While the former is important, it can only be the preliminary to a full moral analysis.

As an analogy, it is useful to consider the relationship between artefacts and athletics. It is indisputable that artefacts influence human athletic performance, in numerous ways: improvements in bike design improve cycling speed, better shoes improve running times, and so on. One might argue that, through Designing this technology, we have "delegated" athletic performance to these artefacts, in the sense that significant portions of particular athletic achievements can be attributed to these artefacts.[12] Nonetheless, no one would argue that we should extend the concept of "athlete" to shoes and bikes, or say that an athlete is not really a human being, but a human being and his bicycle. The reason for this is that, although artefacts shape the context of athletic performance in multiple ways, we are primarily interested not in this, but in human performance itself. In the case of morality, as our primary interest lies in human decision-making, not in the influence of artefacts on it, we have legitimate reason to exclude artefacts from the category of moral agency.

7.5   The Designer Stands Alone?

Whatever we ultimately say on this rather abstruse issue, however, it is important to remember that, even if we cannot extend moral agency, in some meaningful sense or another, to artefacts, we should recognize that they influence the behavior of moral agents to such an extent that they must figure in our moral analyses. Certain artefacts may shape the way people live, and the lives they lead, and make possible certain moral decisions that were otherwise impossible. As discussed in section 1.3, this places tremendous weight on the Designer as an ethical decision-maker. The artefacts she creates will shape the practices and beliefs of, potentially, multiple generations of human beings, often in quite subtle ways that may not even be recognized by those people. Thus we return, at last, to the lonely image, encountered in chapter 2, of the Designer standing over against the massive and intractable task of leading society into the future.

In our earlier encounter with this idea, we viewed it in the context of the so-called "epistemological problem" for Design: the difficulty the Designer has in determining whether or not his novel creation is liable to be successful. The issue of uncertainty regarding consequences arises in the moral context as well (Sollie 2007). But the ethical issue has an additional dimension. For the question confronting the Designer is not simply the empirical question – Will this device do what it is supposed to? – but rather the ethical question – Should there be a device that does this? This shift in the focus of the question does not make it any more straightforward, but only adds a different sort of perplexity. For how is the Designer to decide, as we discussed in section 7.3, what things should do – what people truly need? Which part of the Designer's methodology or training can equip her to answer these normative questions?

There is an important question to be raised here about the true extent of the Designer's responsibility. In chapter 2, we discussed the fact that Designers are typically not given *carte blanche* but are often handed a very specific brief. Many of the ethically relevant aspects of the project may not be up for negotiation; consider a commissioned Design for a hospital, for example. There may be all sorts of ethically important aspects of the project that are simply out of the Designer's control.[13] Perhaps, then, it is society as a whole that should be held responsible, rather than the individual Designer.

However, while it is true that, in given cases, many of the ethically relevant decisions may occur prior to the Design process, it is also true that society increasingly views Design as the proper place for such ethical deliberation to take place. The question is how Design can perform this role.

This question has led to many attempts to find a "formalized approach" for ethical Design, a specific methodology for incorporating values into Design. One of the more prominent of these approaches is "Value Sensitive Design" (VSD; Friedman et al. 2002; Cummings 2006). Value Sensitive Design involves a three-part approach, consisting of conceptual, empirical and technical analyses. The conceptual analysis consists, as one writer puts it, in "an analysis informed by those value constructs relevant to the Design in question" (Cummings 2006, 702). VSD identifies twelve human values that are relevant to Design: human welfare, ownership, privacy, freedom from bias, universal usability, trust, autonomy, informed consent, accountability, calmness, identity and environmental sustainability. In the conceptual phase of VSD, the way in which the Design may impact upon these values, as they are held by the stakeholders affected, is considered. These stakeholders can be either direct stakeholders, who use the Design in question, or indirect stakeholders, who may be indirectly affected by it.

The empirical phase of VSD involves taking measurements and making observations to assess how the Design in question actually affects the relevant human values. In this stage, the focus is on testing how people actually respond to and interact with the Design, and what effects the Design has in actual situations. Finally, the technical phase sees the Designers exploring different ways of implementing their concepts so as to best realize the values identified in the conceptual phase.

Cummings illustrates VSD methodology with the example of a missile guidance system that allows for missile redirection to a new target in mid-flight. In the conceptual phase, human welfare is identified as the main relevant value, and the pertinent issue as "whether an engineer can ethically design a weapon" (2006, 705). This question is addressed by noting that philosophical and legal doctrines of "just war," such as the United Nations Charter, require military actions to be discriminatory, targeting only military and not civilian targets. Since re-directable missiles are "intended to destroy military targets with pinpoint accuracy and thus minimize civilian casualty loss" (706), the Design in question supports the value of human welfare. The main Design issue arising from this Design concept is the level of automation to be implemented in the redirection process: to what extent should redeployment of active ordinance to another target be left to human discretion, and to what extent should automated recommendations for redirection be employed? In the empirical phase, these questions are explored by observing human decisions in prototype systems with varying levels of automation, and in the technical phase ways of implementing automation are considered.

Methodologies such as VSD are certainly useful tools in drawing ethical concerns more fully into the process of Design. However, do they really succeed in addressing the sorts of worries raised above about the Designer's ability to tackle ethical issues? It seems clear that they do not take us far. Manders-Huits (2011) points out a number of important limitations to approaches such as VSD (see also Albrechtslund 2007). One problem involves "how to deal with the . . . empirical investigations concerning values" (2011, 279). In the empirical phase, Designers are to assess how interaction with the Design will affect relevant values. In the missile example, this assessment is relatively straightforward, in that one can measure how many missiles struck unwanted targets. But in many cases, determining how values are affected must be done by asking subjects. These empirical results, however, can be difficult to interpret, as different subjects may understand a value like "autonomy" or "privacy" in very different ways. Furthermore, it is difficult to know what to do with these sorts of empirical results. As Manders-Huits writes: "What does it mean if 67% of the users say that they fear security issues? And do they all refer to the same conception of security? In addition, how does the 67% fear of security problems relate to the 49% fear of privacy issues?" (2011, 279). An even deeper problem with the empirical phase is that these assessments of the values held by different stakeholders are descriptive, rather than normative. Manders-Huits writes, "There is an implicit assumption in the methodology of VSD that one will know what to do in a normative sense, once these values are known. This, I contend, is where VSD runs the risk of committing the naturalistic fallacy" (2011, 279).

An even more fundamental limitation of the VSD approach, however, concerns its conceptual phase. It is in this phase that the relevant values are identified, and the overall ethical direction of the Design project is determined. In Cummings's missile guidance system example discussed above, for example, the ethical question of whether to build this weapon is decided by appealing to an idea within "just war" theory. However, if our aim is to design ethical technology, it is not enough for the technology to align with accepted ethical theories – it should align with *true* ethical theories. Cummings does not argue for the truth of this theory, nor is it at all apparent that Designers would have the capacity to engage with this ethical question. Further, in many cases Designers will face conflict between different values that can be defended by appealing to conflicting ethical theories: the conceptual phase does not indicate how such conflicts can be addressed or resolved. Manders-Huits sums up this line of thought by saying that "VSD requires complimentary ethical theory and expertise" (2011, 282).[14]

These limitations of VSD are important to note, because if such techniques cannot provide a satisfactory answer to the question of *how* Designers are able to do ethics – if, in addition, ethical expertise is required – then the question must inevitably be asked: *who* are Designers to be making these ethical decisions? If the Designer has no particular ethical expertise, his or her ethical decisions are apt to be regarded as arbitrary by the wider community affected by them. The Designer will, of course, have his or her own values – autonomy, privacy, sustainability or whatever – and these may be as sensible as anyone else's values. But the Designer seems no more entitled to "legislate" those values than any other citizen. Yet, this is precisely what happens. This generates a particularly acute difficulty, given that so many of the mediating effects of Design are ones that go unnoticed by users. The Designer, in this context, becomes a shadowy figure quietly foisting her values upon an unsuspecting public.

There are ways to respond to this idea of the Designer as invisible tyrant. One is to insist upon the primacy of agency as a value in Design. In his study of nanotechnology, the philosopher Alfred Nordmann (2005) argues that the *raison d'être* of technology is to increase our control over nature and reduce the extent to which nature operates as a set of unknown background forces beyond our control. Nordmann employs this premise in his critique of nanotechnology, arguing that because the operation of nanotechnology takes place at an imperceptible level, where it is beyond our control, it is flawed technology, reducing rather than enhancing human agency. We might extend Nordmann's analysis to Design in general, arguing that Designers should not create systems that impose actions or ways of perceiving upon users, but only ones that present them with choices for action or perception. This approach would, in a way, allow Designers to dodge the question "Who are *you* to do ethics?" by creating only tools for action. Another way to look at this approach is as an attempt to rein in the mediating effects of Design entities, and restrict them only to effects that leave room for deliberate control and informed consent.

However, this approach is problematic. Designing for agency certainly seems like a good thing in many contexts. However, it is probably not desirable, or even possible, to Design in such a way as to completely avoid imposing values. Some complex devices, at least, might well become unusable if the user had to make conscious decisions about every aspect of their operation. Consider our earlier example of the photocopier: a photocopier with no default settings at all would be so time-consuming to use as to be effectively useless. Thus, it doesn't seem feasible for the Designer to simply dodge the problem in this way.

A second, and related, response to the problem is to endorse some version of the idea of participatory Design.[15] This is the idea that Designers should not create Designs and then make them available to users, but rather that Designers and users co-design, thereby creating an entity that is better adapted to its users. In an ethical context, participatory Design appears to allow the Designer to avoid the sting of the objection, since the Designer does not impose her personal values in the Design she creates: rather, the Design is as much the product of the community of users and their values as it is the product of the Designer and her values. Participatory Design is thereby seen as inherently democratic.

But while the general idea of participatory Design is certainly important and useful in some contexts, it suffers from many of the same limitations that we noted for approaches such as VSD. For instance, it runs the risk of committing the naturalistic fallacy: simply adopting values people actually hold as opposed to engaging in moral analysis. Furthermore, if moral discourse or debate is included in the model, as seems appropriate, then the question of expertise only re-emerges insofar as the qualifications of the public stakeholders are as dubious as those of the Designer herself, if not more so.

An alternative approach would be to say that if the Designer is not, or cannot be, an ethicist, the ethical dimension of her task should be handled by a distinct person, working in conjunction with the Designer.[16] This approach is already employed in certain contexts where "qualified ethicists" (usually philosophers) are involved in systems Design, such as in the Design of health-care protocols. If the ethical problems raised by Design are too much for that practice to resolve, then perhaps ultimately it must be relieved of them.

Epilogue: The Meaning of Modernism

A theme throughout our investigation of Design, and the philosophical issues arising from it, has been the Modernist's attempt to understand the significance of, and the prospects for, the Designer's project. It will then be appropriate to conclude by taking stock of these efforts, and their significance for our own understanding of Design.

The most salient characteristic of Modernism, as Greenhalgh rightly points out, is its tendency to draw connections between different areas. This tendency allowed it to link Design's concerns with how things should be made to larger philosophical issues about how society should be organized and how human beings can best live. Although Modernist thinking brought the key issues of expression, function, aesthetics and consumerism into focus, no philosophy of Design stood ready to take up its analyses in any systematic way. Today, however, we can draw on philosophical theories and analyses from a variety of fields to reconsider the fundamental questions that Modernism raised. While the Modernist's ideas may not survive in their original form, their investigations, more than any others, provide the point around which a true Philosophy of Design might crystalize.

Beyond this, Modernism leaves a larger legacy in terms of its attempt to understand the role of Design in the practices and institutions that constitute the modern world. We saw that the idea of the Designer, as we know it, was born largely of the systems of rationalization, specialization and division of labor that emerged in the industrial revolution. And yet, in the Modernist's eyes, the

Designer was also a hopeful anomaly within those systems. Though the child of rationalization and narrow specialization, the Designer would tame those very forces – a Zeus humbling the Titans – guiding them in the creation of beauty, utility, cultural expression and social good. Although the organic relationship that the craftsperson had with his works, and with his culture, was gone forever, it would be replaced by the organic and synthetic vision of the Designer: the humanist model embodied in the craftsperson's hands would instead be embodied in the Designer's mind. At the center of the industrial system of mass production would be not merely a mashing of institutional gears consisting of experts exercising their narrow brands of formalized rationality, but a human being.

But if this humanist vision is to be more than a Romantic reaction to the disruptions of rationalization – another appeal to ineffable "genius" as savior – Modernism owes us an account of how a human being could tackle the problems that, in this conception, fall on the Designer's shoulders. We have examined how different philosophical strands of Modernist thought try to do this by tracing conceptual connections between notions such as function, beauty, expression and ethics. Whatever we may say about the success of these attempts, we must note the remarkable way in which the Modernist is under constant pressure to break apart the task of the Designer. Expression, for example, is for the most part handed to the artist, and the resolution of ethical dilemmas is parceled out to a new, and as yet only dimly glimpsed, figure, the ethicist. Herein we see a fundamental tension within Modernism itself, as the cold rationality of Loos pulls against the organic humanism of Gropius.

It should not surprise us, in the end, to see the very practice of Design under threat of being torn apart by the forces of rationalization, division of labor, and specialization, for those were the very forces that gave birth to it, even as they destroyed its predecessor, the tradition-based crafts. It is in this context that the efforts of the Modernists continue to command our attention and study. The fundamental question they confront is whether Design can temper the forces that gave it birth, or whether it is no more than a kind of mirage in the ongoing process of specialization, rationalization and fragmentation that characterize the modern world. And that question is every bit as urgent for us today as it was for the Modernist thinkers of 100 years ago.

Notes

Chapter 1   What is Design?

1   As many theorists note, the word "design" is highly ambiguous, referring to, amongst other things, an *activity*, in its verb form, and *things*,
like the Juicy Salif, in its noun form (see Heskett 2005, 3). I focus
here on the verb form as the primary sense, in terms of which the
other senses are to be defined.

2   For more on this notion, see chapter 7 of Gorovitz et al. (1979).

3   For a survey of current discussion surrounding conceptual analysis,
see Margolis and Laurence (1999).

4   Another common argument against the existence of essences, derived
from the writings of Ludwig Wittgenstein, is that when we "look and
see," we simply fail to find them (see Wittgenstein's famous discussion
of games [1953, s. 66]; for an extension of this argument to the case
of art, see Weitz [1956]). Skeptics such as Forsey can hardly appeal
to *this* argument, however, since there have hardly been any attempts
to find the relevant definition for design!

5   This approach is taken even further by John Dilworth, who argues
that "a design is some configuration that (to competent observers) *can
be regarded as if* a designer might have intentionally produced it,
whether or not it was so produced" (2001, 171; my emphasis).

6   Distinct from this, and more plausible, is the claim that we all design
some of the time. Donald Norman asserts this claim with respect to
interior decoration: "When consciously, deliberately rearranging
objects on our desks, the furniture in our living rooms, and the things
we keep in our cars, we are designing" (2005, 224).

7 See the *Oxford English Dictionary*, entry for the verb "design," II.b. This sense is described as "archaic and rare," though not obsolete. The verb entered English around 1400 from French and Italian cognates ultimately derived from the Latin *designare*, which meant "to signify or mark out."

8 I have added "intentional": on the need for this modification, see Bamford (1990, 229–38). I have also dropped Jones's reference to change "in man-made things," which would arbitrarily rule out landscape design, at least when carried out on previously unmodified natural areas, and design in fields such as synthetic biology (Ginsberg 2014; compare also Forsey 2013, 34n32). Related definitions are offered by, among others, Herbert Simon ("everyone designs who devises course of action aimed at changing existing situations into preferred ones" [Simon 1996, 111]); Nigel Cross ("We all design when we plan for something new to happen" [2011, 3]); and John Heskett ("Design, stripped to its essence, can be defined as the human capacity to shape and make our environment in ways without precedent in nature, to serve our needs and give meaning to our lives" [2005, 5]).

9 Another of *The Oxford English Dictionary*'s definitions for the verb "design" is "to make plans for the production of a device according to . . . structural or functional criteria" (III.15). This definition correctly captures the fact that design is the creation of a plan, but fails to specify that the plan must be for something of a novel *type* (creating a plan for a Mission-style bed at 7/8 scale, for example, would not be designing).

10 "Building on paper" is an established part of architectural practice and some such "buildings" have an important place in the history of architecture (the structures in Sant'Elia's sketches, for example; see Banham 1960, 127–37).

11 Some reject the idea that design is problem solving; I consider this position in section 2.4.

12 Houkes and Vermaas (2010, 26) define designing as the construction of "use plans," which are sequences of actions whereby one does something with an object. This way of describing it has the advantage, as they point out, of emphasizing that design does not simply produce a new thing, but something that one can do (with that thing). That is, things are made not for their own sake, but as a means of solving some problem or achieving some goal.

13 Although the definition refers to a singular designer, nothing in this account implies that design is a solo activity; it could be, and often is, a highly collaborative process. The extent to which this must be the case, as we will see in chapter 2, turns out to be one of the central issues a philosophy of design has to consider.

14   For a different view, perhaps, compare Pye (1978), who claims that
     "as everyone knows, it is possible to design things that cannot be
     made" (19).
15   Compare a definition of "design" employed by Galle (2008): "produc-
     tion of representations according to an idea, so as to enable a maker
     to produce an artefact that the designer will recognize as being in
     accordance with his idea." Insofar as failed designs are not "in accord-
     ance" with the designer's idea, this definition rules out the possibility
     of design failure (for a more recent definition of design by Galle,
     however, see Galle 2011, 93). For discussion of some complexities in
     what counts as "failed design," see Kroes (2002, 299ff.).
16   An accessible introduction to ontology is Loux (2002); a comprehen-
     sive survey of recent work in ontology is Loux and Zimmerman
     (2003). Galle (2008) discusses ontology in the context of design.
17   One might object that we can't conceive this, since cats obviously
     need food, water and air to live – so how could there possibly be only
     a cat, without any of these other things? However, the sense of pos-
     sibility required here is only *logical possibility*: something is logically
     possible just in case its description does not involve a contradiction.
     Even though a universe consisting of a single cat violates the laws of
     nature as we understand them, it does not seem to involve a logical
     contradiction, as a concept like "round square" does. Another way to
     put it is that, if the laws of nature were different than we know them
     to be, then a single cat *could* exist, whereas the same is not true of a
     round square.
18   Along similar lines, Houkes and Vermaas (2010) distinguish "plan
     designing" (30) from product designing, where only the latter leads
     to a new material object (2010, 26); see also Galle (2008, 273).
19   In her account of the aesthetics of design, Forsey takes up this issue,
     and appears to defend something akin to the singularity view: "with
     design, it is the physical artefact with all of its apparent qualities
     that is the candidate for our aesthetic evaluation" (2013, 53). In
     support of this view, she points to the tentative or preliminary char-
     acter of design plans: "[This] element I think we can exclude, in
     part because we do not normally see or have access to a designer's
     proposals. An artist may make preliminary sketches of a paint-
     ing . . . but we do not normally consider these to be finished 'works'
     in themselves" (21; see also 53). However, while we may not typically
     appreciate plans or sketches, we do appreciate types, which are
     not preliminary or provisional in the way that rough sketches or
     plans are.
20   The distinction between architecture and "mere building" is famously
     made by Pevsner (1942).

21 Perhaps it is such differences in intention that lead us to see the build-
     ing constructed in Nashville in 1897, according to the plans of the
     Athenian Parthenon, as merely a copy of the Parthenon, and not
     another one.

22 Another example is Eero Saarinen's Gateway Arch in St. Louis, which
     is one element of his larger design for the Jefferson National Expansion
     Memorial surrounding it.

23 Designs might also be made singular by incorporating particular
     times as well as particular things: for example, the design of an
     opening ceremony for an Olympic games might be realizable only
     on one occasion, with any subsequent production being merely a
     re-enactment of the original.

24 The distinction at issue here has sometimes been suppressed by theo-
     rists. Herbert Simon, for example, proposed that the traditional pro-
     fessions, including law, medicine, education, business and so on, are
     all design professions (1996). His aim in doing this was to highlight
     similarities between the professions, and suggest that there are effec-
     tive methods common to all of them. But whether or not Simon's
     grouping of all the professions together is illuminating and helpful,
     it remains a fact that we also recognize distinctions, such as the one
     at issue, between them.

25 Hamilton draws here on David Pye's (1978) conception of design as
     necessarily involving a concern for more than mere functionality;
     Pye's idea will be discussed further in section 6.1.

26 Forsey takes a position similar to mine in stating that we should not
     confuse the question of what design is with the question of how we
     should appreciate or evaluate it (2013, 18). Whether Forsey follows
     her own advice, however, is unclear, for she goes on to reject the view
     that designs are types on the grounds that "it is the physical artifact
     with all its apparent qualities that is the candidate for our aesthetic
     evaluation" (2013, 53; see also 34n32).

27 Note that "mere" social practices need not be any less important than
     the more prestigious professions: parenting, for example, is a social
     practice, and by any reckoning is one of the most important activities
     in any culture.

28 Some deny that theoretical science's primary aim is to explain the
     world, on the grounds that our best-supported scientific theories
     ought not to be regarded as true. Even on this empiricist view,
     however, the primary aim of theoretical science is to allow us to
     predict the course of nature, not to alter it.

29 Of course, they each do this in quite different ways. We should also
     note that art's primary aim can shift to the practical, as when a novel
     endorses certain forms of action, or when an environmental artwork

produces ecological benefits. But in these cases, the shift to the practical makes it natural to reclassify the works as cases of design rather than "art": as propaganda, in the first example, and as landscape architecture in the second.

30   Bamford classifies engineering among the Design professions (1990); common practice, however, recognizes a distinction between the two (Molotch 2003). As Stan Swallow, co-creator of a "smart fabric" vest for the British military put it, "Sometimes I'm a scientist, sometimes I'm an engineer, and sometimes I'm a designer."

31   A similar notion is Krippendorff's idea of "second order understanding," for which "designers need to understand the position from which their stakeholders understand the world" (2006). None of this is to say that Designers do not *consider* broader issues – as we will see in chapter 2, they do. But what they *create* is the surface.

32   This feature of Design will also distinguish Designers from legislators, whose design activity, for better or worse, appears more akin to engineering.

33   Craft has often been used, as I am using it here, as a stalking horse of sorts for theories of Design (Jones 1970, ch. 2, and Alexander 1964, chapter 4), and also for theories of art (a classic discussion is Collingwood 1938, 15–17). Although tradition-based craft is one kind of craft, it is certainly not definitive of craft in general; for a more comprehensive view of contemporary craft, and its overlap with art and design, see Shiner (2012) and also the essays in Dorner (1997).

Chapter 2   The Design Process

1   Here I construe "function" as restricted to matters that are "practical," in the usual sense of that word; thus I distinguish functionality from concerns such as self-expression and aesthetics. As we will see in chapter 5, the notion of function is far from unproblematic.

2   Some of these general constraints on successful Design solutions are discussed by Houkes and Vermaas (2010, ch. 2). For example, solutions must solve the problem without thwarting our other goals or aims, they should not require means that are unavailable to us, and so on.

3   In her recent account of Design, Forsey seems to reject the symbolic dimension of Design problems altogether, insisting that Design objects are "mute," "say nothing" and cannot be interpreted (i.e., said to have meaning) (2013, 64). Forsey does not claim that all Design objects lack meaning, but offers this as a general statement about most Design. Whether this is true as a description of most contemporary Design,

however, is highly questionable; as we'll see in chapter 4, a wide body of contemporary analysis assumes that everyday Design objects do have meaning. More importantly, Forsey's decision to discuss only "mute" Design objects completely obscures the normative question of whether Design *should* be expressive. As will be discussed in chapter 4, this is one of the central issues for the philosophy of Design.

4 This point is made by Simon (1996, 150–1) who suggests that Design's conception of "the client" has broadened to include more than the corporate employer who foots the bill. Along similar lines, David Pye remarks that "the designer has a responsibility to far more people than those who pay him and those who use his designs" (1978, 94).

5 Houkes and Vermaas refer to "goal-adjustment" (2010, 31).

6 Simon (1996, 113). Simon focuses on engineering, but he also applies his criticisms to fields relevant to Design in our sense, such as architecture, medicine and business (111).

7 In one sense, Designers often "justify" their Designs by explaining why they have the particular features they do. When asked "Why is this here?," the Designer responds by describing the intended function of the part or aspect in question. The sense of "justify" relevant to our discussion here is a stronger one, however: to have justification is not just to have a reason for including the various aspects in the Design, but to have a good reason to think those aspects will solve the original Design problem.

8 Galle describes the problem as "the reliability problem" (2011, 94n73); he suggests some responses in Galle (2008).

9 On the trial-and-error adaptation of tradition-based craft, see chapter 2 of Jones (1970), and chapter 4 of Alexander (1964).

10 It is worth noting that the epistemological problem for Design is not the more general epistemological problem of induction: the problem of induction is the problem of how *any evidence* can support a claim about an unobserved event, such as the sun's rising tomorrow. Even if we had a solution to this general problem, we would still have the problem of finding evidence to support the Designer's confidence in his novel solutions.

11 Note that this holds only for certain theories of art; if the goal of art is, say, the *communication* of emotion from the artist to an audience, as argued by Tolstoy ([1898] 1995), rather than merely the expression of the artist's emotion, something akin to the Designer's problem again arises.

12 All references employ the standard Stephanus numbers used in scholarly editions.

13 Tatarkiewicz ([1962–7] 2005, 28–9). Plato discusses this conception of poetry in the dialogue *Ion*.

14　In the psychological literature, creativity is often defined more broadly, as the ability to conceive an idea that is "both original and *appropriate*" (Howard et al. 2008, 172; my emphasis). This entails that a theory of creativity must address the epistemological problem for Design by explaining how Design ideas can be known to be "appropriate"; such theories typically do so by allowing for the empirical testing of Design solutions, a response I consider below. For further discussion of the philosophical issues involved in defining "creativity," see Gaut (2010).

15　An example of this approach in architecture is the set of Designs presented by Christopher Alexander and his colleagues in their well-known book *A Pattern Language*. Of these designs, they write that "each pattern may be looked upon as a hypothesis like one of the hypotheses of science" (Alexander et al. 1977, xv); for criticism of these "hypotheses," see Protzen (1980). For discussion of a rather different take on how Design might be thought to succeed by following the "scientific method," see Bamford (2002).

16　See also Houkes and Vermaas, who write: "As long as [designers'] belief in the effectiveness of the communicated use plan is justified, e.g., on the basis of extensive tests, such designing can be evaluated as rational" (2010, 43).

17　Some "Darwinian" theories of Design acknowledge this difference between Darwinian natural selection and Design practice, and so are not really "Darwinian" at all (see, e.g., Rutter and Agnew 1998, who provide a list of criteria for "good designs"). On the other hand, truly Darwinian accounts of Design do portray Design solutions as random and uncertain, even if they do not fully acknowledge the consequences of this (see, e.g., Langrish, who writes that "the best designer in the world has no way of knowing what the future will bring" [2004, 12]; see also Brey 2008).

18　Whether or not these "epistemic virtues" have any connection to the truth of a hypothesis has long been a central question in the philosophy of science, but even those who deny such a connection see explanatory power as a virtue of scientific hypotheses (see, e.g., Van Fraassen 1980).

19　Schön characterizes Design as a kind of know-how, but one with an additional element of "reflection in action," whereby the Designer "turns thought back on action and on the knowing which is implicit in action" (1983, 50). In doing this, he "reflects on the understandings which have been implicit in his action, understandings which he surfaces, criticizes, restructures, and embodies in further action" (50). This method, Schön claims, "is central to the art through which practitioners sometimes cope with the troublesome 'divergent situations of practice'" (62). However, while this kind of reflection may be an important element of Design know-how, it does not help to address the epistemological problem for Design, since without a connection to some actual experience of the efficacy of the Design, such reflection would amount to no more than speculation.

Chapter 3   Modernism

1   The classic historical account of the origins of Modernism in Design, originally published in 1936, is Pevsner (1936] 2011); also influential is Banham (1960). For overviews of recent work, see Sparke (2004) and Lees-Maffei and Houze (2010).
2   A classic source for this idea of the ongoing "rationalization" of industrial society is the work of Max Weber (1904–5).
3   See, for example, Marx's discussion of the effects of the division of labor in *The German Ideology* ([1846] 1983, 73–83).
4   Grosz ([1911] 1975, 47). On Morris's reaction to the poor quality of goods at the London Great Exhibition of 1851, see Pevsner ([1936] 2011).
5   On the notion of rational reconstruction, see Carnap (1962); for defense of it in the context of Design, see Houkes and Vermaas (2010, 22–6).
6   Tournikiotis (1994, 23) disputes the usual 1908 publication date of the essay, arguing that although Loos lectured on the subject in Vienna in 1910, the work was first published, in French, in 1920.
7   Graham (2003) suggests that Loos's rejection of ornament is based on "a horror of deception" and/or a desire that architecture not involve two distinct phases of construction and ornament. Neither of these readings seems to me straightforwardly supported by Loos's text, though, as we will see in chapter 4, the idea of deception plays an important role in Modernist thinking about ornament.
8   For a similar line of thought, compare Le Corbusier's discussion of Breton furniture ([1931] 1986, 138–40).
9   As is often pointed out, the home interiors that Loos himself Designed were far from plain, a fact that contradicts this strident rejection of ornament. Loos's considered view, which isn't apparent in "Ornament and crime," appears to have been that *certain forms* of ornament were acceptable in contemporary urban culture, a more moderate position held by earlier writers on ornament, notably Owen Jones (1856). Nonetheless, the more radical position of "Ornament and crime" was more influential than this more modest one, and came to be associated with Loos's name.

10   A variant of this extreme position is adopted by Forsey, who restricts Design to "mute" objects that have no meaning or content (2013, see section 2.1, especially n3 above). Forsey adopts this approach so as to mark a starker contrast between Design and art, which, in her view, characteristically has meaning or content. But such theoretical considerations do not justify simply ignoring a major element of Design as we know it.

11   Despite its claims of breaking with the past, Modernism admired and took much from classical ideas. See, for example, Le Corbusier's admiration of the Parthenon (1931), and note 12 on Loos below.

12   Loos illustrates his view using the example of ancient Greek pottery ([1898b] 1982, 35–7).

13   This remark is attributed to Socrates in the *Greater Hippias* (295d), a dialogue often attributed to Plato. For further discussion of this view, see Tatarkiewicz ([1962–7] 2005, 100–4).

14   On the growing aesthetic appreciation of mechanical engineering in the nineteenth century, in particular the iron bridge, see chapter 5 of Pevsner ([1936] 2011). On eighteenth-century philosophical debates concerning the idea that what is functional is beautiful, see chapter 1 of Parsons and Carlson (2008).

15   Another classic celebration of machine beauty is Le Corbusier's discussion of the automobile ([1931] 1986, 133–48). The machine aesthetic and related ideas will be discussed further in chapter 6.

16   The slogan originated with the American architect Louis Sullivan, who was an important influence on the development of Modernism. Like Loos, however, Sullivan was by no means opposed to all ornamentation; for a statement of his views, see Sullivan ([1892] 1975).

17   These changes were not the product of pure theory, however – they were also tied to technological innovations in production techniques and materials, and in some cases to economic considerations (Sparke 2004).

18   Pruitt–Igoe's legacy remains controversial, however; for a defense of the project, see Bristol (1980).

19   Another important critique of Modernism, already mentioned earlier, is Scruton's rejection of Modernist architecture. Unlike the writers under discussion, however, Scruton does not conclude from the supposed failure of Modernist architecture that the notion of good Design itself is undermined.

20   This is a familiar criticism of Modernism in general: Joyce's novels, for example, were said to be deliberately obscure so that they could not be understood by the ordinary reader. Interestingly, however, whereas Modernism in literature and painting made forms

too complex for the popular taste, Modernism in Design apparently made them too simple.

21 On the influence of Modernist ideas on Apple design, see Isaacson (2011). In contrast to the notion of an artistic classic, the idea of the "Design classic" is complicated by the fact that some Designs fall from favor, not because of any defect, but due to external factors, such as social or technological changes that make them obsolete. We can, however, think of Design classics not only as Designs that stay in demand, but Designs that exert an influence on subsequent Designs. Thus, for example, the Anglepoise lamp, though no longer widely produced, exerted a great influence on the subsequent styling of desk lighting (Parsons 2013).

Chapter 4 Expression

1 The literature in this area is vast, and crosses many disciplines; for a recent overview, see Hicks and Beaudry (2010).

2 A further complexity arises from the fact that, as Daniel Miller (1987) points out, quite different forces can be at play in different kinds of consumer goods: houses may be very different from cheap disposable consumer items, for instance.

3 Many theoretical accounts simply ignore this crucial point. Krippendorff (2006), for example, notes that people buy cars, clothes and similar items for their symbolic meaning, not their utility, and declares that "meaning matters more than function" is therefore an "axiom" for Design (47–9).

4 A classic discussion of the Greek concept of *eros* is Plato's *Symposium*, in which not only bodies but decidedly non-sexual things, such as customs, laws and philosophical ideas, are all described as objects of *eros* (210–12).

5 Loos develops this idea through a rather acerbic comparison of the clothing habits of the English and those of his fellow Viennese; the latter dress to stand out, but are really all the same, whereas the English behave as individuals, despite their uniform appearance ([1919] 2011, 73–6).

6 As mentioned above, in this chapter I consider the rejection of ornament only insofar as it relates to expression; in chapter 6, I will examine the idea of aesthetic ornamentation.

7 Of course, here again one might think of confounding factors, such as the pleasant relaxation that one gets from a leisurely stroll, but not from the faster trip by bicycle.

8   This premise is relevant to a counter-example to the Better Realization Argument suggested by Victor Bruzzone. He points out that verbal expression of our thoughts is superior to communication using bodily expression, or "body language." However, it would be highly unintuitive to conclude that we ought therefore not to regard expressiveness (facial expressions, for example) as a good-making feature of bodies. People with no bodily expressiveness would strike us as bizarre, or inhuman. However, in this case we can identify a "spin-off benefit" of the use of body language. For we are emotional creatures, and emotions are to a significant degree (though not exclusively) experienced in the body, so that bodily expression serves to effectively communicate emotion in a way that purely verbal communication cannot.

9   Irving Singer (1966) explores the way that illusions allow people to "create their own universe" in the context of romantic love.

10 Here again there emerges an interesting connection between Modernist ideas and the classical tradition; compare the contrast drawn by Hamilton (1930) between the plain, realistic aesthetic of ancient Greek art and the highly ornamental and fantastical tendencies of other cultures.

11 The famous exception is Plato, some of whose objections to poetry were discussed in chapter 2.

12 Some does, at least, but of course certain genres (Hollywood movies, for example) are heavily constrained by an analogous set of factors.

Chapter 5   The Concept of Function

1   It should be noted that Millikan introduced "proper function" as a term of art, and stipulated its meaning (in line with a view that I will discuss in section 5.3 below). She intended the notion to do theoretical work in the philosophy of mind and language, and explicitly denied that her notion of proper function is meant to account for our everyday usage of the term "function" (see Millikan 1984, 1989). More specifically, Millikan's project, generally known as *teleosemantics*, was to use the idea of proper function to provide a naturalistic account of the meaning of words and mental states (on this project, see Neander 2012). My concern here is different; I use "proper function" to designate a familiar concept that we seek to explicate.

2   Excellent surveys of the literature in this area are Preston (2009) and Houkes and Vermaas (2010, ch. 3).

3   Although Pye rejects talk of function, he stresses the role of "intended results" in understanding Design (1978, 18).

4   Intentionalist theories of artefact function are developed by Searle (1995), Dipert (1993), Kitcher (1993), McLaughlin (2001) and Neander (1991). Intentionalist accounts that explicitly apply to proper function are given by Griffiths (1993), Millikan (1984, 1999) and Houkes and Vermaas (2004, 2010).

5   The argument given below is based upon Preston (1998, 2003).

6   The evolutionary theory, as presented here, has roots in Wright (1973) but is fully developed for both biological and artefactual functions, by Millikan (1984, 1999). A useful development of this theory, in regard to the biological case, is Godfrey-Smith (1994).

7   This formulation is by Parsons and Carlson (2008, 75), but the idea is due to Preston (1998).

8   This theory of function thus overlaps with so-called "Evolutionary theories of technology," which draw a similar analogy between artefacts and organisms. These theories are often developed as historical accounts of technological change (see, e.g., Basalla 1988); for a philosophical survey of these theories, see Brey (2008).

9   This isn't always clear from accounts of the etiological theory: Parsons and Carlson (2008), for example, describe the theory they endorse as selectionist, but in fact this isn't the case.

10 Preston (1998, 2003), notably, rejects any role for intentions, adopting instead a pluralist theory that combines the etiological theory of proper function and a theory of "system function," based on the ideas of Robert Cummins (1975).

11 For a critical discussion of this approach, see Nanay (2010). Vermaas and Houkes (2003) raise the point that, although this account requires the members of a family to be similar, some artefact kinds are "rather varied in appearance and basic mechanism." Their example is paper-clips: "some consist of nested U-turns, others of two little connected metal plates" (278). They claim that this would require us to distinguish two different types. Even if this is the case, however, this does not seem problematic for the evolutionary theory: in fact, we do distinguish these two artefactual kinds: stationery stores sell the latter as "binder clips," not paper-clips.

12 In her earlier account (1998), Preston herself adopted this approach.

13 Preston makes a large generalization here, but gives only the commodity example to support it. Even this example doesn't fit her claim as well as one might like, since – complaints of rampant commercialism notwithstanding – much of material culture is not actually a commodity (think of trash, memorabilia, works of art and so on).

14 We can also note that this explanation need not entail that *feng shui* mirrors allow practitioners to *believe* that their homes are healthier: practitioners need not believe this (although I suspect many

practitioners do believe this). Rather, *feng shui* mirrors may simply make them *feel* as though their environment is healthier, because they were brought up in environments influenced by *feng shui*, or because of their attachment to tradition, or whatever.

15   This problem regarding novel artefacts is a version of the infamous "swampman" problem for Millikan's teleosemantics: on Millikan's view, particular mental states (beliefs, for example) have content in virtue of what their ancestors did. But this implies that a creature atom-for-atom identical to you, formed due to a mere random assembly of molecules (a "swampman"), would not believe or desire anything (see Neander 2012).

16   She also notes that the evolutionary theorist is not prevented from explicating the functions of novel artefacts in some other way, by adopting a different theory of function: such functions will simply not be *proper* functions (see also Parsons and Carlson 2008, 83).

17   See also Preston (2013). Longy argues that, in general, there is no clear-cut answer as to whether we have a "new artefact" (2009, 64–5).

18   A similar issue arises regarding Modernism's "Form follows Function" dictum. One might wonder whether the etiological theory would imply that form automatically or trivially follows function, since to have a function at all an object must possess the character shared by artefacts of that type. But merely possessing this character is hardly enough to ensure a fit of form to function: an awkward, heavy shovel is still a shovel, but not one whose form really follows its function.

Chapter 6   Function, Form and Aesthetics

1   A similar idea is Preston's "multiple realizability of function": "any function can ordinarily be realized in a variety of materials and/or forms" (2013, 135); see also the discussion of Kant's notion of dependent beauty in section 6.3 below.

2   Color can be functional in some cases, of course, as when objects are brightly colored to enhance visibility for safety reasons. The general lack of connection between function and color is emphasized by Brett (2005).

3   The word "beauty" is used in different senses in these debates: although it is sometimes contrasted with the notion of aesthetic value, I will use the two terms synonymously here. My survey of different theories of beauty or aesthetic value will be selective: for a wider discussion see Shelley (2013).

4 This set of ideas in the popular imagination also, as it turns out, reflects the early history of philosophical thinking about beauty: see Stolnitz (1961).

5 Stolnitz himself insisted that the two attitudes were not mutually exclusive (1961, 45), but this is, I believe, an error generated by his belief that there are two distinct kinds of attention: practical and disinterested (see the discussion of Dickie's critique below).

6 This aspect of Levinson's view is rooted in an influential idea of Frank Sibley's: the idea that aesthetic properties are not "condition-governed," in an important sense. Sibley wrote, "There are no sufficient conditions, no non-aesthetic features such that the presence of some set or number of them will beyond question justify or warrant the application of an aesthetic term" (1959, 426). Levinson's idea is that, since no description of the non-aesthetic properties (colors and shapes, for example) of an object will entail that it has any aesthetic property, we have to regard aesthetic properties as something more than those non-aesthetic properties: they must be "real" properties in their own right. It is important to note, however, that Sibley himself was primarily concerned with understanding the workings of aesthetic *language*, and not with ontological questions concerning the "reality" of aesthetic properties.

7 In other words, aesthetic properties are "response-dependent," or "secondary" qualities; on the analogy with color, see Sibley ([1968] 2001), and the discussion of Hume (1757) below.

8 "Dependent beauty" is also sometimes translated as "adherent beauty," but I use the former, more well-established, term here.

9 Note, however, that Guyer (2002a) also endorses a more positive interpretation of Kant's conception of dependent beauty, which he sees as compatible with this earlier interpretation.

10 Wicks's recourse to this notion is partly an attempt, on his part, to capture an element of Kant's account of beauty, the so-called "free play of the faculties of imagination and understanding." Wicks, quite naturally, interprets "imagination" as involving the production of mental images, but for a criticism of this as an interpretation of Kant, see Guyer (1999).

11 This point is often neglected. Shiner, for example, writes, "When it comes to the exterior appearance . . . it would seem impossible to determine which forms are 'standard' today . . . for many . . . building types . . . so that Walton's categories are of limited value in arriving at an . . . aesthetic judgement" (2011, 35). In response to Shiner's complaint, Sauchelli (2013) suggests that we reject a Walton-style account in favor of one that focuses on our expectations. However, this focus on expectations is already implicit in Walton's account.

12 Walton writes that "a work's aesthetic properties depend on its non-aesthetic properties; the former are 'emergent' . . . I take this to be true of all the examples of aesthetic properties we will be dealing with" (1970, 337–8). This point is sometimes neglected, however; De Clercq (2013) and Ross (2009), for example, imply that such accounts aim to provide sufficient conditions for the presence of an aesthetic property.

13 Originally, Parsons and Carlson suggested that this aesthetic property was characterized by an object's having only standard properties; for a critique, see De Clercq (2013).

14 Walton observes that features can be *too* standard, but holds that, generally, standardness does contribute to this aesthetic quality of rightness, necessity or unity.

15 Rachel Zuckert describes an interpretation of dependent beauty along similar lines, holding that things possess dependent beauty when their properties are "pleasing in their evocative connections or reciprocal play with the object's . . . function" (2007, 207). On this view, features like the spoilers and fins on a sportscar might give it dependent beauty, insofar as they "evoke" its function of going fast.

16 De Clercq (2013) argues that this type of functional beauty arises from the simultaneous occurrence of looking fit and looking unfit. Whether that is the case or not, this still counts as a distinct form of functional beauty as we experience it.

17 A sophisticated version of this view would hold not that such statements are *about* the preferences of the speaker, but rather that they *express* them; for a general discussion of such views in ethics, see chapter 3 of Miller (2003).

18 In ethics, one strategy for "explaining away" dispute of this kind is to appeal to a desire on the part of speakers to have others adopt one's preferences and aversions. However, this strategy fails in the aesthetic case, as Kivy (1980) points out, since there is no parallel motivation for seeking an alignment of *aesthetic* preferences.

19 Some would reject the idea that anything is "naturally fitted" to produce pleasure in everyone, holding that things are praised as beautiful only because they speak to certain social, economic or cultural preferences. Against this view, Hume appeals to the existence of works that stand the test of time. Since these works (the poems of Homer, for example) have pleased in every age and culture, their appeal cannot be explained by their meshing with particular social, economic or cultural preferences.

20 An influential recent discussion of this issue is by Levinson (2002), who calls it the "real problem of Taste." Something like the same

problem, however, can be discerned in earlier commentators, including Ducasse (1966).

21 The solution given below is a greatly abridged version of the one given by Levinson (2002); I place much more emphasis on the role of Mill's test. Hume's own answer to this "problem" (which he did not note himself) seems to have turned on the inherent value of "delicacy of sentiment": "It is acknowledged to be the perfection of every sense or faculty, to perceive with exactness its most minute objects, and allow nothing to escape its notice and observation . . . a delicate taste of wit or beauty must always be a desirable quality . . . In this decision the sentiments of all mankind are agreed. Wherever you can ascertain a delicacy of taste, it is sure to meet with approbation" ([1757] 2006, 351–2; see Wieand 2003).

Chapter 7 Ethics

1 For an overview of the general area of ethics and Design, see the relevant essays in Berg Olsen et al. (2009) and Meijers et al. (2009). Other issues in this area, not discussed in this chapter, include the analogy between the practice of solving Design problems and moral reasoning (see Whitbeck 1998; Dorst and Royakkers 2006; and van Amerongen 2004), the relationship between aesthetic and ethical values in Design (Saito 2007) and Design's role in producing tools for teaching or developing ethics (Lloyd and van de Poel 2008). Another area of research not covered here is the application of particular philosophical approaches to ethics to the realm of Design; see, for example, D'Anjou (2010).

2 As a less extreme example, consider the recent development of smart-phone apps that allow you to purchase restaurant reservations from a third party. Since the system works by clogging restaurants with blocks of phony reservations, which are then sold at a profit, many view the app as inherently unethical insofar as it leaves proprietors with empty seats that they cannot fill.

3 Classic discussions of technological determinism are Ellul (1980) and Heilbroner (1967); for recent discussions, see Dusek (2006) and Wyatt (2009).

4 The Modernist might object that these things are all desired, ultimately, for expressivist or aesthetic reasons. While this *may* be the case, however, it *needn't* be. To claim that anyone who wanted a leaf blower, for example, wanted it for expressivist or aesthetic reasons would be to make a sweeping a priori claim about motivations. It is

perfectly conceivable that someone wants a leaf blower to merely blow leaves around!

5   For a refreshingly blunt engagement with it, however, see the comments by Philippe Starck in Leberecht (2008).

6   See also Herbert Marcuse, who says that "'false' needs are those which are superimposed upon the individual by particular social interests in his repression" (1964, 4–5).

7   Something like this point is captured in Frankfurt's remark that, with false needs, "there is no necessity except what is created by the desire" (1984, 12).

8   Here again, we can mark an interesting contrast with the arts, for it is generally not true that merely to make a work of art is to endorse some conception of the good life. For discussion of how Designers might envision "the good life," see Swierstra and Waelbers (2012), and also Borgmann (1984).

9   It is worth noting, however, that even if the Designer decides on the needs of others, it need not be the case that, as Le Corbusier put it, "All men have the same needs" ([1931] 1986, 136); on the contrary, if what we need is tied to what will make good come to be or allow us to avoid evil, as Aristotle put it, then we should expect our needs to be highly dependent upon the particular circumstances in which we find ourselves.

10   For a general overview of issues relating to moral responsibility in computing ethics, see Noorman (2014).

11   Note that, while Floridi and Sanders do not believe that moral responsibility is necessary for moral agency, they do hold that other characteristics are. Agents must be interactive with their environment, autonomous (able to alter their operation in a way that isn't directly dependent upon interaction with the environment) and adaptable, or able to alter their operation in response to interaction with the environment. The argument given by Floridi and Sanders would only allow us to say that entities that are interactive, autonomous and adaptable are moral agents. This would cover sophisticated computer devices, but certainly not more mundane artefacts such as speed bumps and overpasses, to which Winner and Latour wanted to grant moral agency. These lack not only moral responsibility, but also other morally salient qualities of moral agents, such as the ability to act freely and intentionally.

12   In some cases, the contributions that these artefacts make to performance can even be quantified precisely – as an effect of aerodynamic bike modifications on cycling times, for instance.

13   This point can be made with regard to production of Design objects as well as their use, when aspects of production have ethical significance.

14 Even if we set aside the truth of the ethical axioms appealed to in the conceptual phase, there is still a further problem in the claim that a particular Design will support those axioms (Albrechtslund 2007). For example, Cummings finds that these missile guidance systems support "just war" doctrine, and hence human welfare, because they allow for more precise military strikes. But technology that allows for more discriminatory attacks could just as easily be used to selectively destroy or threaten civilian targets. For example, an army could dispatch an ultimatum to an enemy leader and then publicly announce the launch of missiles at civilian targets. If the leader concedes to the ultimatum, the missiles would be retargeted. In this way, such a system could be used as a tactic for terrorizing civilian populations.

15 On this topic, see Spinuzzi (2005); Feng (2000); see also the essays in a special issue of *Design Studies* on Participatory Design: **28** (3) 2007.

16 Along these lines, see the suggestion by Manders-Huits and Zimmer (2009) that Design teams include a "values advocate" (see also Cummings 2006).

Suggestions for Further Reading

The philosophical literature drawn on in this book is spread across a number of subfields of philosophy, chiefly aesthetics, applied ethics, the philosophy of technology, and the philosophy of science. In aesthetics, excellent guides to the literature are Gaut and Lopes (2013) and Levinson (2003); many relevant studies appear in the *Journal of Aesthetics and Art Criticism* and the *British Journal of Aesthetics*. Work on the aesthetics of architecture is particularly salient: for a recent overview of work in this area see De Clercq (2012). Studies dealing with Design more broadly include Saito (2007), Parsons and Carlson (2008) and Forsey (2013). The field of environmental aesthetics also touches on many issues relevant to Design: for an overview, see Parsons (2012). In applied ethics, the journal *Ethics and Engineering Sciences* covers many relevant issues. Much work in the philosophy of technology intersects with Design issues: a concise introduction to the field is Dusek (2006). Verbeek (2008), Houkes and Vermaas (2010) and Preston (2013) are in-depth philosophical studies of material artefacts that delve deeply into key issues for Design; Verbeek (2011) is an excellent guide to ethical issues that go beyond the framework of applied ethics. The online journal *Techné: Research in Philosophy and Technology* contains many articles of interest. Finally, within the field of Design itself, the journals *Design Studies* and *Design Issues* have a theoretical rather than a philosophical focus, but contain many relevant contemporary studies. Much classic material in Design theory is usefully collected in Clark and Brody (2009).

References

Albrechtslund, A. (2007) Ethics and technology design. *Ethics and Information Technology* **9**, 63–72.

Alexander, C. (1964) *Notes on the Synthesis of Form*. Cambridge, MA: Harvard University Press.

Alexander, C. (1971) The state of the art in design methodology. *DMG Newsletter* **5**, 3–7.

Alexander, C., Ishikawa, S., Silverstein, M., Jacobsen, M., Fiksdahl-King, I. and Angel, S. (1977) *A Pattern Language*. New York: Oxford University Press.

Alexander, C. and Poyner, B. (1970) The atoms of environmental structure. In G. Moore (ed.) *Emerging Methods in Environmental Design and Planning*. Cambridge, MA: MIT Press, pp. 308–21.

Archer, B. (1979) Whatever became of design methodology? *Design Studies* **1**, 17–20.

Aristotle (1971) *Aristotle's Metaphysics: Books Γ, Δ, and E*, trans. C. Kirwan. Oxford: Clarendon Press.

Bakker, W. and Loui, M. (1997) Can designing and selling low-quality products be ethical? *Science and Engineering Ethics* **3**, 153–70.

Bamford, G. (1990) Design, science, and conceptual analysis. In J. Plume (ed.) *Architectural Science and Design in Harmony: Proceedings of the Joint ANZAScA/ADTRA Conference, Sydney, July 10–12, 1990*. Australia & New Zealand Architectural Science Association, pp. 229–38.

Bamford, G. (2002) From analysis/synthesis to conjecture/analysis: a review of Karl Popper's influence on design methodology in architecture. *Design Studies* **23**, 245–61.

Banham, R. (1960) *Theory and Design in the First Machine Age*. London: The Architectural Press.

Barthes, R. [1957] (1972) *Mythologies*, trans. A. Lavers. New York: Hill and Wang.

Basalla, G. (1988) *The Evolution of Technology*. Cambridge: Cambridge University Press.

Bayazit, N. (2004) Investigating design: a review of forty years of design research. *Design Issues* **20**, 16–29.

Beardsley, M. (1958) *Aesthetics: Problems in the Philosophy of Criticism*. New York: Harcourt, Brace & World.

Beardsley, M. (1982) Aesthetic experience. In M. Wreen and D. Callen (eds.) *The Aesthetic Point of View: Selected Essays*. Ithaca: Cornell University Press, pp. 285–97.

Berg Olsen, J., Pedersen, S. and Hendricks, V. (eds.) (2009) *A Companion to the Philosophy of Technology*. Oxford: Blackwell.

Borgmann, A. (1984) *Technology and the Character of Contemporary Life*. Chicago: University of Chicago Press.

Bourdieu, P. (1984) *Distinction: A Social Critique of the Judgement of Taste*, trans. R. Nice. Cambridge, MA: Harvard University Press.

Brett, D. (2005) *Rethinking Decoration: Pleasure & Ideology in the Visual Arts*. Cambridge: Cambridge University Press.

Brey, P. (2008) Technological design as an evolutionary process. In P. Vermaas, P. Kroes, A. Light and S. Moore (eds.) *Philosophy and Design: From Engineering to Architecture*. Dordecht: Springer, pp. 61–76.

Bristol, K. (1980) The Pruitt-Igoe myth. *Journal of Architectural Education* **44**, 163–71.

Brolin, B. (1976) *The Failure of Modern Architecture*. New York: Van Nostrand Reinhold.

Buchanan, R. (1992) Wicked problems in design thinking. *Design Issues* **8**, 5–21.

Buller, D. (1998) Etiological theories of function: a geographical survey. *Biology and Philosophy* **13**, 505–27.

Campbell, C. (1989) *The Romantic Ethic and the Spirit of Consumerism*. Oxford: Blackwell Publishers.

Campbell, C. (2010) What is wrong with consumerism? An assessment of some common criticisms. *Anuario Filosófico* **63**, 279–96.

Carnap, R. (1962) *The Logical Foundations of Probability*, 2nd edn. Chicago: University of Chicago Press.

Clark, H. and Brody, D. (eds.) (2009) *Design Studies: A Reader*. Oxford: Berg Publishers.

Collingwood, R. (1938) *The Principles of Art*. Oxford: Clarendon Press.

Coyne, R. (2005) Wicked problems revisited. *Design Studies* **26**, 5–17.

Croce, B. [1902] (1922) *Aesthetic as Science of Expression and General Linguistic*, trans. D. Ainslie. New York: Noonday Press.

Cross, N. (2011) *Design Thinking*. Oxford: Berg.

Cummings, M. (2006) Integrating ethics in design through the value-sensitive design approach. *Science and Engineering Ethics* **12**, 701–15.

Cummins, R. (1975) Functional analysis. *Journal of Philosophy* **72**, 741–65.

D'Anjou, P. (2010) Toward an horizon in design ethics. *Science and Engineering Ethics* **16**, 355–70.

Danto, A. (1981) *The Transfiguration of the Commonplace: A Philosophy of Art*. Cambridge, MA: Harvard University Press.

Davies, S. (2003) Ontology of art. In J. Levinson (ed.) *Oxford Handbook of Aesthetics*. Oxford: Oxford University Press, pp. 155–80.

De Clercq, R. (2012) Architecture. In A. Ribeiro (ed.) *The Continuum Companion to Aesthetics*. London: Continuum, pp. 210–14.

De Clercq, R. (2013) Reflections on a sofa bed: functional beauty and looking fit. *Journal of Aesthetic Education* **47**, 35–48.

Dickie, G. (1964) The myth of the aesthetic attitude. *American Philosophical Quarterly* **1**, 56–65.

Dickie, G. (1974) *Art and the Aesthetic: An Institutional Analysis*. Ithaca: Cornell University Press.

Dickie, G. (1984) *The Art Circle*. New York: Haven Publications.

Dilworth, J. (2001) Artworks versus designs. *British Journal of Aesthetics* **41**, 162–77.

Dipert, R. (1993) *Artifacts, Art Works, and Agency*. Philadelphia: Temple University Press.

Dorner, P. (ed.) (1997) *The Culture of Craft: Status and Future*. Manchester: Manchester University Press.

Dorst, K. and Royakkers, L. (2006) The design analogy: a model for moral problem solving. *Design Issues* **27**, 633–56.

Dorst, K. and Vermaas, P. (2005) John Gero's function-behaviour-structure model of designing: a critical analysis. *Research in Engineering Design* **16**, 17–26.

Douglas, M. and Isherwood, B. (1979) *The World of Goods*. New York: Basic Books.

Ducasse, C. (1966) *The Philosophy of Art*. New York: Dover.

Dusek, V. (2006) *Philosophy of Technology: An Introduction*. Oxford: Wiley Blackwell.

Eco, U. (2005) *History of Beauty*, trans. A. McEwen, 2nd edn. New York: Rizzoli.

Ellul, J. (1980) *The Technological System*, trans. J. Neugrosschel. New York: Continuum.

Ewald, K. [1925–6] (1975) The beauty of machines. In T. Benton, C. Benton and D. Sharp (eds.) *Architecture and Design, 1890–1939: An International Anthology of Original Articles*. New York: Whitney Library of Design, pp. 144–6.

Feng, P. (2000) Rethinking technology, revitalizing ethics: overcoming barriers to ethical design. *Science and Engineering Ethics* **6**, 207–20.

Floridi, L. and Sanders, J. (2004) On the morality of artificial agents. *Minds and Machines* **14**, 349–79.

Forsey, J. (2013) *The Aesthetics of Design*. Oxford: Oxford University Press.

Forty, A. [1986] (2005) *Objects of Desire: Design and Society since 1750*. London: Thames and Hudson.

Frankfurt, H. (1984) Necessity and desire. *Philosophy and Phenomenological Research* **45**, 1–13.

Friedman, B., Kahn, P. and Borning, A. (2002) Value Sensitive Design: Theory and Methods. UW CSE Technical Report, University of Washington, Seattle.

Galle, P. (2008) Candidate worldviews for design theory. *Design Studies* **29**, 267–303.

Galle, P. (2011) Foundational and Instrumental design theory. *Design Issues* **27**, 81–94.

Gaut, B. (2010) The philosophy of creativity. *Philosophy Compass* **5**, 1034–46.

Gaut, B. and Lopes, D. (eds.) (2013) *The Routledge Companion to Aesthetics*, 3rd edn. London: Routledge.

Gero, J. and Kannengiesser, U. (2004) The situated function-behaviour-structure framework. *Design Studies* **25**, 373–91.

Ginsberg, D. (2014) Design as the machines come to life. In D. Ginsberg, J. Calvert, P. Schyfter, A. Elfick and D. Endy (eds.) *Synthetic Aesthetics: Investigating Synthetic Biology's Designs on Nature*. Cambridge, MA: MIT Press, pp. 39–72.

Godfrey-Smith, P. (1994) A modern history theory of functions. *Noûs* **28**, 344–62.

Goffman, E. (1959) *The Presentation of the Self in Everyday Life*. New York: Anchor Books.

Gorovitz, S., Hintikka, M., Provence, D. and Williams, R. (1979) *Philosophical Analysis: An Introduction to its Language and Techniques*, 3rd edn. New York: Random House.

Graham, G. (2003) Architecture. In J. Levinson (ed.) *Oxford Handbook of Aesthetics*. Oxford: Oxford University Press, pp. 555–71.

Greenhalgh, P. (1990) Introduction. In P. Greenhalgh (ed.) *Modernism in Design*. London: Reaktion Books, pp. 1–24.

Greenhalgh, P. (1997) The history of craft. In P. Dormer (ed.) *The Culture of Craft*. Manchester: Manchester University Press, pp. 20–52.

Greenough, H. (1853) American architecture. In H. Tuckerman (ed.) *A Memorial of Horatio Greenough, Consisting of a Memoir Selections from his Writings and Tributes to his Genius*. New York: G. P. Putnam and Co., pp. 117–30.

Gregory, S. (ed.) (1966) *The Design Method*. London: Butterworth Press.

Griffiths, P. (1993) Functional analysis and proper functions. *British Journal for the Philosophy of Science* **44**, 409–22.

Grillo, P. (1960) *Form, Function, and Design*. Toronto: General Publishing Company.

Gropius, W. (1965) *The New Architecture and the Bauhaus*, trans. P. Morton Shand. Cambridge, MA: MIT Press.

Grosz, K. [1911] (1975) Ornament. In T. Benton, C. Benton and D. Sharp (eds.) *Architecture and Design, 1890–1939: An International Anthology of Original Articles*. New York: Whitney Library of Design, pp. 46–8.

Guyer, P. (1979) *Kant and the Claims of Taste*. Cambridge, MA: Harvard University Press.

Guyer, P. (1999) Dependent beauty revisited: a reply to Wicks. *Journal of Aesthetics and Art Criticism* **57**, 357–61.

Guyer, P. (2002a) Free and adherent beauty: a modest proposal. *British Journal of Aesthetics* **42**, 357–66.

Guyer, P. (2002b) Beauty and utility in eighteenth-century aesthetics. *Eighteenth-century Studies* **35**, 439–53.

Haapala, A. (2005) On the aesthetics of the everyday: familiarity, strangeness, and the meaning of place. In A. Light and J. Smith (eds.) *The Aesthetics of Everyday Life*. New York: Columbia University Press, pp. 39–55.

Hamilton, A. (2011) The aesthetics of design. In J. Wolfendale, J. Kennett and F. Allhoff (eds.) *Fashion: Philosophy for Everyone, Thinking with Style*. New York: Wiley-Blackwell, pp. 53–69.

Hamilton, E. (1930) *The Greek Way*. New York: W. W. Norton & Co.

Harris, D. (2001) *Cute, Quaint, Hungry and Romantic: The Aesthetics of Consumerism*. Cambridge, MA: De Capo Press.

Heilbroner, R. (1967) Do machines make history? *Technology and Culture* **8**, 335–45.

Heskett, J. (2005) *Design: A Very Short Introduction*. Oxford: Oxford University Press.

Hicks, D. and Beaudry, M. (2010) Introduction: material culture studies: a reactionary view. In D. Hicks and M. Beaudry (eds.) *The Oxford Handbook of Material Culture Studies*. Oxford: Oxford University Press, pp. 1–21.

Hillier, B. and Leaman, A. (1974) How is design possible? *Journal of Architectural and Planning Research* **3**, 4–11.

Hillier, B., Musgrove, J. and O'Sullivan, P. (1972) Knowledge and design. In W. Mitchell (ed.) *Environmental Design: Proceedings of the era/ar8 Conference, University of California at Los Angeles, January 1972*. Los Angeles: University of California Press, 29-3-1–29-3-14.

Hilpinen, R. (2011) Artifact. In E. Zalta (ed.) *Stanford Encyclopedia of Philosophy*. Winter 2011 Edition; http://plato.stanford.edu/archives/win2011/entries/artifact.

Hine, T. (1986) *Populuxe*. New York: Knopf.

Houkes, W. and Vermaas, P. (2004) Actions versus functions: a plea for an alternative metaphysics of artifacts. *The Monist* **87**, 52–71.

Houkes, W. and Vermaas, P. (2010) *Technical Functions: On the Use and Design of Artefacts*. Dordrecht: Springer.

Howard, T., Culley, S. and Dekoninck, E. (2008) Describing the creative design process by the integration of engineering design and cognitive psychology literature. *Design Studies* **29**, 160–80.

Hume, D. [1757] (2006) Of the standard of taste. In G. Sayre-McCord (ed.) *David Hume: Moral Philosophy*. Indianapolis: Hackett, pp. 345–60.

Idhe, D. (2008) The designer fallacy and technological innovation. In P. Vermaas, P. Kroes, A. Light and S. Moore (eds.) *Philosophy and Design: From Engineering to Architecture*. Dordecht: Springer, pp. 51–60.

Irwin, T. (1989) *Classical Thought*. Oxford: Oxford University Press.

Isaacson, W. (2011) *Steve Jobs*. New York: Simon & Schuster.

Jencks, C. (1991) *The Language of Post-Modern Architecture*, 6th edn. New York: Rizzoli.

Jens, H. (2009) Fashioning uniqueness: mass customization and the commoditization of identity. In H. Clark and D. Brody (eds.) *Design Studies: A Reader*. Oxford: Berg Publishers, pp. 326–35.

Johnson, D. (2006) Computer systems: moral entities but not moral agents. *Ethics and Information Technology* **8**, 195–204.

Jones, C. (1965) Systematic design methods and the building design process. *Architects' Journal* **22**, 685–7.

Jones, C. (1970) *Design Methods: Seeds of Human Futures*. London: Wiley-Interscience.

Jones, C. (1977) How my thoughts about design methods have changed during the years. *Design Methods and Theories* **11**, 48–62.

Jones, O. (1856) *The Grammar of Ornament*. London: Day and Son.

Kant, I. [1790] (2001) *Critique of the Power of Judgment*, trans. P. Guyer and E. Matthews. Cambridge: Cambridge University Press.

Kitcher, P. (1993) Function and design. *Midwest Studies in Philosophy* **18**, 379–97.

Kivy, P. (1980) A failure of aesthetic emotivism. *Philosophical Studies* **38**, 351–65.

Klein, N. (1999) *No Logo*. New York: Picador USA.

Korsmeyer, C. (2013) Taste. In B. Gaut and D. Lopes (eds.) *The Routledge Companion to Aesthetics*, 3rd edn. London: Routledge, pp. 257–66.

Krippendorff, K. (2006) *The Semantic Turn: A New Foundation for Design*. Boca Raton: Taylor and Francis Group.

Kroes, P. (2002) Design methodology and the nature of technical artefacts. *Design Studies* **23**, 287–302.

Langrish, J. (2004) Darwinian design: the memetic evolution of design ideas. *Design Issues* **20**, 4–19.

Latour, B. (1992) Where are the missing masses? The sociology of a few mundane artifacts. In W. Bijker and J. Law (eds.) *Shaping Technology / Building Society: Studies in Sociotechnical Change*. Cambridge, MA: MIT Press, pp. 225–58.

Lawson, B. (2004) *What Designers Know*. Boston: Elsevier / Architectural Press.

Leberecht, T. (2008) Philippe Starck and "design is dead." *CNET Magazine*. Available from www.cnet.com/news/philippe-starck-and -design-is-dead.

Le Corbusier [1931] (1986) *Towards a New Architecture*, trans. F. Etchells. London: The Architectural Press.

Lees-Maffei, G. (2010) New designers, 1676–1820: introduction. In G. Lees-Maffei and R. Houze (eds.) *The Design History Reader*. Oxford: Berg, pp. 13–14.

Lees-Maffei, G. and Houze, R. (eds.) (2010) *The Design History Reader*. Oxford: Berg.

Levinson, J. (1984) Aesthetic supervenience. *Southern Journal of Philosophy* **22S**, 93–110.

Levinson, J. (1994) Being realistic about aesthetic properties. *Journal of Aesthetics and Art Criticism* **52**, 351–4.

Levinson, J. (2001) Aesthetic properties, evaluative force and differences of sensibility. In E. Brady and J. Levinson (eds.) *Aesthetic Concepts: Essays after Sibley*. Oxford: Clarendon Press, pp. 61–80.

Levinson, J. (2002) Hume's standard of taste: the real problem. *Journal of Aesthetics and Art Criticism* **60**, 227–38.

Levinson, J. (ed.) (2003) *Oxford Handbook of Aesthetics*. Oxford: Oxford University Press.

Lloyd, P. and van de Poel, I. (2008) Designing games to teach ethics. *Science and Engineering Ethics* **14**, 433–47.

Loewy, R. (1988) *Industrial Design*. New York: Overlook Press.

Longy, F. (2009) How biological, cultural, and intended functions combine. In U. Krohs and P. Kroes (eds.) *Functions in Biological and Artificial Worlds*. Cambridge, MA: MIT Press, pp. 51–67.

Loos, A. [1898a] (1982) Furniture for sitting. In *Spoken into the Void*, trans. J. Newman and J. Smith. Cambridge, MA: MIT Press, pp. 29–33.

Loos, A. [1898b] (1982) Glass and clay. In *Spoken into the Void*, trans. J. Newman and J. Smith. Cambridge, MA: MIT Press, pp. 35–7.

Loos, A. [1898c] (2011) Ladies fashion. In *Why a Man Should Be Well-Dressed: Appearances Can Be Revealing*, trans. M. Troy. Vienna: Metroverlag, pp. 62–70.

Loos, A. [1908] (1970) Ornament and crime. In U. Conrads (ed.) (1970) *Programs and Manifestoes on 20th-Century Architecture*. Trans. M. Bullock. Cambridge, MA: MIT Press, pp. 19–24.

Loos, A. [1919] (2011) The English uniform. In *Why a Man Should be Well-Dressed: Appearances Can be Revealing*, trans. M. Troy. Vienna: Metroverlag, pp. 73–6.

Lopes, D. (2007) Shikinen Sengu and the ontology of architecture in Japan. *Journal of Aesthetics and Art Criticism* **65**, 77–84.

Loux, M. (2002) *Metaphysics: A Contemporary Introduction*. New York: Psychology Press.

Loux, M. and Zimmerman, D. (eds.) (2003) *The Oxford Handbook of Metaphysics*. Oxford: Oxford University Press.

Love, T. (2002) Constructing a coherent cross-disciplinary body of theory about designing and designs: some philosophical issues. *Design Studies* **23**, 345–61.

Lovell, S. (2011) *Dieter Rams: As Little Design as Possible*. Phaidon Press.

MacCarthy, F. (1995) *William Morris: A Life for Our Time*. New York: Knopf.

Manders-Huits, N. (2011) What values in design? The challenge of incorporating moral values into design. *Science and Engineering Ethics* **17**, 271–87.

Manders-Huits, N. and Zimmer, M. (2009) Values and pragmatic action: the challenges of introducing ethical intelligence in technical design communities. *International Review of Information Ethics* **10**, 37–44.

Marcuse, H. (1964) *One-Dimensional Man: Studies in the Ideology of Advanced Industrial Society*. Boston: Beacon Press.

Margolis, E. and Laurence, S. (eds.) (1999) *Concepts: Core Readings*. Cambridge, MA: MIT Press.

Marx, K. [1846] (1983) The German ideology. In E. Kamenka (ed.) *The Portable Karl Marx*. New York: Penguin, pp. 162–96.

McLaughlin, P. (2001) *What Functions Explain: Functional Explanation and Self-Reproducing Systems*. Cambridge: Cambridge University Press.

Meijers, A., Gabbay, D. M. and Woods, J. (eds.) (2009) *Philosophy of Technology and Engineering Sciences*. Oxford: Elsevier.

Michl, J. (1995) Form follows what? The modernist notion of function as a carte blanche. [Online] *Magazine of the Faculty of Architecture and Town Planning* **10**. Available from www.geocities.com/Athens/2360/jm-eng .fff-hai.html.

Mill, J. S. [1861] (1979) *Utilitarianism*, ed. G. Sher. Indianapolis: Hackett.

Miller, A. (2003) *An Introduction to Contemporary Metaethics*. Cambridge: Polity.

Miller, D. (1987) *Material Culture and Mass Consumption*. Oxford: Blackwell.

Millikan, R. (1984) *Language Thought and Other Biological Categories*. Cambridge, MA: MIT Press.

Millikan, R. (1989) In defense of proper functions. *Philosophy of Science* **56**, 288–302.

Millikan, R. (1999) Wings, spoons, pills and quills: a pluralist theory of function. *Journal of Philosophy* **96**, 191–206.

Molotch, H. (2003) *Where Stuff Comes From: How Toasters, Toilets, Cars, Computers and Many Other Things Come to Be as They Are*. New York: Routledge.

Mumford, L. (1934) *Technics and Civilization*. n.p.: Harcourt.

Nanay, B. (2010) A modal theory of function. *Journal of Philosophy* **8**, 412–31.

Neander, K. (1991) The teleological notion of "function." *Australasian Journal of Philosophy* **69**, 454–68.

Neander, K. (2012) Teleological theories of mental content. In E. Zalta (ed.) *Stanford Encyclopedia of Philosophy*. Spring 2012 Edition; http://plato.stanford.edu/archives/spr2012/entries/content-teleological.

Neeley, K. and Luegenbiehl, H. (2008) Beyond inevitability: emphasizing the role of intention and ethical responsibility in engineering design. In P. Vermaas, P. Kroes, A. Light and S. Moore (eds.) *Philosophy and Design: From Engineering to Architecture*. Dordecht: Springer, pp. 247–58.

Nelson, H. and Stolterman, E. (2012) *The Design Way: Intentional Change in an Unpredictable World*, 2nd edn. Cambridge, MA: MIT Press.

Noorman, M. (2014) Computing and moral responsibility. In E. Zalta (ed.) *Stanford Encyclopedia of Philosophy*. Summer 2014 Edition; http://plato.stanford.edu/archives/sum2014/entries/computing-responsibility.

Nordmann, A. (2005) *Noumenal* technology: reflections on the incredible tininess of nano. *Techné: Research in Philosophy and Technology* **8**, 3–23.

Norman, D. (1988) *The Psychology of Everyday Things*. New York: Basic Books.

Norman, D. (2005) *Emotional Design: Why We Love (or Hate) Everyday Things*. New York: Basic Books.

Papanek, V. (1971) *Design for the Real World: Human Ecology and Social Change*. New York: Pantheon Books.

Parsons, G. (2011) Fact and function in architectural criticism. *Journal of Aesthetics and Art Criticism* **69**, 21–9.

Parsons, G. (2012) Environmental aesthetics. In A. Ribeiro (ed.) *The Continuum Companion to Aesthetics*. London: Continuum, pp. 228–41.

Parsons, G. (2013) Design. In B. Gaut and D. Lopes (eds.) *The Routledge Companion to Aesthetics*, 3rd edn. London: Routledge, pp. 616–26.

Parsons, G. and Carlson, A. (2008) *Functional Beauty*. Oxford: Oxford University Press.

Petroski, H. (2006) *Success through Failure: The Paradox of Design*. Princeton: Princeton University Press.

Pevsner, N. [1936] (2011) *Pioneers of Modern Design: From William Morris to Walter Gropius*, 4th edn. Bath: Palazzo.

Pevsner, N. (1942) *An Outline of European Architecture*. New York: Penguin.

Plato (1997) *Collected Works*, ed. J. Cooper. Indianapolis: Hackett.

Postrel, V. (2003) *The Substance of Style: How Aesthetic Value is Remaking Commerce, Culture, and Consciousness*. New York: HarperCollins Publishers.

Preston, B. (1998) Why is a wing like a spoon? *Journal of Philosophy* **95**, 215–54.

Preston, B. (2003) Of marigold beer – a reply to Vermaas and Houkes. *British Journal for the Philosophy of Science* **54**, 601–12.

Preston, B. (2009) Philosophical theories of artifact function. In A. Meijers, D. Gabbay and J. Woods (eds.) *Philosophy of Technology and Engineering Science*. Oxford: Elsevier, pp. 213–33.

Preston, B. (2013) *A Philosophy of Material Culture: Action, Function, and Mind*. New York: Routledge.

Protzen, J. (1980) The poverty of the pattern language. *Design Studies* **1**, 291–8.

Protzen, J. and Harris, D. (2010) *The Universe of Design, Horst Rittel's Theories and Design and Planning*. London: Routledge.

Pye, D. (1978) *The Nature and Aesthetics of Design*. Bethel: Cambium Press.

Rawsthorn, A. (2008) What is good design? *The New York Times*, 6 June.

Rittel, H. and Webber, M. (1973) Dilemmas in a general theory of planning. *Policy Sciences* **4**, 155–69.

Ross, S. (2009) Review of *Functional Beauty*. *Notre Dame Philosophical Review* July.

Rutter, B. and Agnew, J. (1998) A Darwinian theory of good design. *Design Management Journal* **9**, 36–41.

Ryle, G. (1946) Knowing how and knowing that. *Proceedings of the Aristotelian Society* **46**, 1–14.

Saito, Y. (2007) *Everyday Aesthetics*. Oxford: Oxford University Press.

Sauchelli, A. (2013) Functional beauty, perception, and aesthetic judgements. *British Journal of Aeshetics* **53**, 41–53.

Schellekens, E. (2012) Aesthetic properties. In A. Ribeiro (ed.) *The Continuum Companion to Aesthetics*. London: Continuum, pp. 84–97.

Schön, D. (1983) *The Reflective Practitioner. How Professionals think in Action*. New York: Basic Books / Harper Collins.

Schön, D. (1988) Designing: rules, types and worlds. *Design Studies* **9**, 181–90.

Schorske, C. (1980) *Fin-De-Siècle Vienna: Politics and Culture*. New York: Alfred A. Knopf.

Schwartz, P. (1999) Proper function and recent selection. *Philosophy of Science* **66** (Proceedings), S210–22.

Scott, G. [1914] (1999) *The Architecture of Humanism: A Study in the History of Taste*. New York: W. W. Norton & Co.

Scruton, R. (1979) *The Aesthetics of Architecture*. Princeton: Princeton University Press.

Scruton R. (1994) *The Classical Vernacular: Architectural Principles in an Age of Nihilism*. New York: St. Martin's Press.

Scruton, R. (2011) A bit of help from Wittgenstein. *British Journal of Aesthetics* **51**, 309–19.

Searle, J. (1995) *The Construction of Social Reality*. New York: The Free Press.

Selle, G. (1984) There is no kitsch, there is only design! *Design Issues* **1**, 41–52.

Sharpe, R. (2004) *Philosophy of Music: An Introduction*. Montreal and Kingston: McGill-Queen's University Press.

Shelley, J. (2013) The concept of the aesthetic. In E. Zalta (ed.) *Stanford Encyclopedia of Philosophy*. Fall 2013 Edition; http://plato.stanford.edu/archives/fall2013/entries/aesthetic-concept.

Shelley, P. [1840] (1988) A defence of poetry. In D. Clark (ed.) *Shelley's Prose*. London: Fourth Estate, pp. 275–97.

Shiner, L. (2011) On aesthetics and function in architecture. *Journal of Aesthetics and Art Criticism* **69**, 31–41.

Shiner, L. (2012) "Blurred boundaries?" Rethinking the concept of craft and its relation to art and design. *Philosophy Compass* **7**, 230–44.

Sibley, F. (1959) Aesthetic concepts. *Philosophical Review* **68**, 421–50.

Sibley, F. [1968] (2001) Objectivity and aesthetics. In J. Benson, B. Redfern and J. Cox (eds.) *Approach to Aesthetics: Collected Papers on Philosophical Aesthetics*. Oxford: Clarendon Press, pp. 71–87.

Simon, H. (1996) *The Sciences of the Artificial*, 3rd edn. Cambridge, MA: MIT Press.

Singer, I. (1966) *The Nature of Love*. Cambridge, MA: MIT Press.

Sollie, P. (2007) Ethics, technology development and uncertainty: an outline for any future ethics of technology. *Journal of Information, Communication & Ethics in Society* **5**, 293–306.

Sparke, P. (2004) *An Introduction to Design and Culture: 1900 to the Present*, 2nd edn. London: Routledge.

Spinuzzi, C. (2005) The methodology of participatory design. *Technical Communication* **52**, 163–74.

Stecker, R. (2003) Aesthetic experience and aesthetic value. *Philosophy Compass* **1**, 1–10.

Stolnitz, J. (1960) *Aesthetics and Philosophy of Art Criticism: A Critical Introduction*. Boston: Houghton Mifflin Company.

Stolnitz, J. (1961) "Beauty": some stages in the history of an idea. *Journal of the History of Ideas* **22**, 185–204.

Sullivan, L. [1892] (1975) Ornament in architecture. In T. Benton, C. Benton and D. Sharp (eds.) *Architecture and Design, 1890–1930: An International Anthology of Original Articles*. New York: Whitney Library of Design, pp. 2–4.

Swierstra, T. and Waelbers, K. (2012) Designing a good life: a matrix for the technological mediation of morality. *Science and Engineering Ethics* **18**, 157–72.

Tatarkiewicz, W. [1962–7] (2005) *History of Aesthetics, Volume I: Ancient Aesthetics*, trans. A. Czerniawski and A. Czerniawski. London: Continuum.

Tolstoy, L. [1898] (1995) *What is Art?* trans. R. Pevear and L. Volokhonsky. London: Penguin.

Tournikiotis, P. (1994) *Adolf Loos*, trans. M. McGoldrick. New York: Princeton Architectural Press.

Van Amerongen, M. (2004) The moral designer. *Techné: Research in Philosophy and Technology* **7**, 112–25.

Van de Poel, I. (2009) Values in engineering design. In A. Meijers, D. M. Gabbay and J. Woods (eds.) *Philosophy of Technology and Engineering Sciences*. Oxford: Elsevier, pp. 973–1006.

Van Fraassen, B. C. (1980) *The Scientific Image*. Oxford: Oxford University Press.

Van Gorp, A. and van de Poel, I. (2008) Deciding on ethical issues in engineering design. In P. Vermaas, P. Kroes, A. Light and S. Moore (eds.) *Philosophy of Design: From Engineering to Architecture*. Dordrecht: Springer, pp. 77–90.

Veblen, T. [1899] (1994) *The Theory of the Leisure Class*. New York: Dover.

Venturi, R., Brown, D. and Izenour, S. (1977) *Learning from Las Vegas*, 2nd edn. Cambridge, MA: MIT Press.

Verbeek, P.-P. (2005) *What Things Do: Philosophical Reflections on Technology, Agency, and Design*, trans. R. Crease. University Park, PA: Pennsylvania State University Press.

Verbeek, P.–P. (2008) Morality in design: design ethics and the morality of technological artifacts. In P. Vermaas, P. Kroes, A. Light and S. Moore (eds.) *Philosophy and Design: From Engineering to Architecture*. Dordecht: Springer, pp. 91–104.

Verbeek, P.-P. (2011) *Moralizing Technology: Understanding and Designing the Morality of Things*. Chicago: University of Chicago Press.

Vermaas, P. and Houkes, W. (2003) Ascribing functions to technical artefacts: a challenge to etiological accounts of functions. *British Journal for the Philosophy of Science* **54**, 261–89.

Vincente, K., Burns, C. and Pawlak, W. (1997) Muddling through wicked design problems. *Ergonomics in Design* **5**, 25–30.

Walker, J. (1989) *Design History and the History of Design*. London: Pluto Press.

Walton, K. (1970) Categories of art. *Philosophical Review* **79**, 334–67.

Wang, J., Joy, A. and Sherry, J. (2013) Creating and sustaining a culture of hope: feng shui discourses and practices in Hong Kong. *Journal of Consumer Culture* **13**, 241–63.

Weber, M. [1904–5] (1958) *The Protestant Ethic and the Spirit of Capitalism*, trans. T. Parsons. New York: Charles Scribner's Sons.

Weitz, M. (1956) The role of theory in aesthetics. *Journal of Aesthetics and Art Criticism* **15**, 27–35.

Whitbeck, C. (1998) *Ethics in Engineering Practice and Research*. Cambridge: Cambridge University Press.

Wicks, R. (1994) Architectural restoration: resurrection or replication? *British Journal of Aesthetics* **34**, 163–9.

Wicks, R. (1997) Dependent beauty as the appreciation of teleological style. *Journal of Aesthetics and Art Criticism* **55**, 387–400.

Wieand, J. (2003) Hume's real problem. *Journal of Aesthetics and Art Criticism* **61**, 395–8.

Wiggins, D. and Derman, S. (1987) Needs, need, needing. *Journal of Medical Ethics* **13**, 62–8.

Wilde, O. [1891] (2003) *The Picture of Dorian Gray*. New York: Penguin.

Wingler, H. (1962) *The Bauhaus – Weimar, Dessau, Berlin, Chicago*. Cambridge, MA: MIT Press.

Winner, L. (1980) Do artifacts have politics? In *The Whale and the Reactor: A Search for Limits in an Age of High Technology*. Chicago: University of Chicago Press, pp. 19–39.

Wittgenstein, L. (1953) *Philosophical Investigations*, trans. E. Anscombe. Oxford: Basil Blackwell.

Wolfe, T. (1981) *From Bauhaus to Our House*. New York: Farrar Straus Giroux.

Wright, L. (1973) Functions. *Philosophical Review* **82**, 139–68.

Wyatt, S. (2009) Technological determinism is dead: long live technological determinism. In E. Hackett, O. Amsterdamska, M. Lynch and J. Wajcman (eds.) *The Handbook of Science and Technology Studies*. Cambridge, MA: MIT Press, pp. 165–80.

Zebrovitz, L. (1997) *Reading Faces: Window to the Soul?* Boulder: Westview Press.

Zuckert, R. (2007) *Kant on Beauty and Biology: An Interpretation of the Critique of Judgment*. Cambridge: Cambridge University Press.

Index

advertising   94, 137–8
Aesthetic (Art for Art's Sake)
    Movement   57
aesthetic aspect of Design   29, 45,
    52, 62, 67, 116
aesthetic attitude   107–9
aesthetic experience   109–10
aesthetic pleasure   20, 66,
    110–11, 119, 125
    see also Taste, problem of
aesthetic properties   111–12, 116
    see also functional beauty
aesthetic realism see aesthetic
    properties
aesthetics of the
    everyday   110–11
aesthetic value
    in definition of Design   19–20
    in Design problems see aesthetic
        aspect of Design
    dispute over see Taste, problem
        of   123
    incompatible with
        function   103–12
    Modernist view of   62–3

theories of see aesthetic attitude;
    aesthetic experience; aesthetic
    realism; aesthetics of the
    everyday; dependent beauty;
    Dickie, G.; functional beauty
Alexander, C.   31, 32, 33–4, 45,
    101, 106, 158n33, 159n9,
    160n15
ancestry   96
anthropology   71–2, 75
Apple   4, 68
applied ethics   130–3
Archer, B.   34
architecture   9, 21, 23, 25–6, 48,
    50, 81
    "building on paper"   155n10
    landscape   158n29
    and "mere buildings"   15
    Modernist   61–2, 64–5 162n19
    nineteenth-century   80
    ontology of   15–18
    see also Gropius; Le Corbusier;
        Libeskind; Loos; Pevsner;
        Sant'Elia; Sullivan; Wright,
        Frank Lloyd